THE
FENG SHUI BIBLE

THE DEFINITIVE GUIDE TO IMPROVING YOUR LIFE, HOME, HEALTH, AND FINANCES

Simon Brown

STERLING
New York

STERLING and the distinctive Sterling logo are
registered trademarks of Sterling Publishing Co., Inc.

20   19   18   17   16   15

Published by Sterling Publishing Co., Inc.
1166 Avenue of the Americas, New York, NY 10036

© Octopus Publishing Group 2005
Text © Simon Brown 2005

Distributed in Canada by Sterling Publishing Co., Inc.
c/o Canadian Manda Group, 664 Annette Street
Toronto, Ontario, Canada M6S 2C8

First published in Great Britain in 2005
by Godsfield Press, a division of
Octopus Publishing Group Ltd
Carmelite House, 50 Victoria Embankment
London EC4Y 0DZ
www.octopusbooksusa.com

Manufactured in China

ISBN 978-1-4027-2983-6

CONTENTS

Feng shui basics 6

The Building blocks of feng shui 64

The Feng shui directory 94

    Feng shui and your home 104

    Feng shui and your health 124

    Feng shui and your moods 146

    Feng shui and your relationships 170

    Feng shui and your creativity 198

    Feng shui and your finances 226

    Feng shui and moving home 248

    Feng shui and your family 276

    Feng shui and your career 308

    Feng shui and nature 328

    Feng shui and your spiritual life 350

Glossary 384

Index 389

About the author 398

Acknowledgements 400

FENG SHUI ☯

BASICS

INTRODUCTION

Use feng shui to create the best atmosphere for your family to thrive.

Despite its current popularity, feng shui is not a new phenomenon – since ancient times people have harnessed the forces of nature and the earth's energy to improve their environment and their way of life. Today, when life throws up so many challenges, it is essential to get the forces of nature working with you, rather than against you, so that you can achieve your full potential and create the most positive atmosphere in which to succeed -- and this is where feng shui provides so many answers.

Feng shui has become a major phenomenon around the world – used by all strata of society, from famous celebrities and major corporations to the family living down the road – because intuitively it makes sense: you feel better and operate at your full capacity in the right atmosphere. More importantly, you will quickly see that feng shui really works and can help to improve not only your home and your immediate environment, but also your health and moods, your relationships, creativity, finances and family life, career and spiritual life.

Here are some of the other improvements that you might experience after using feng shui:

• Greater control of your own destiny

• A better understanding of life

• A happier atmosphere at home

• A greater awareness of the forces of nature

• The ability to create an environment that helps you to achieve your full potential.

Feng shui is not about magic solutions -- it is about developing yourself in a way that gives you the means to draw in the power around you and live your life to the full.

How to benefit from this book

The knowledge contained in this book will make it possible for you to live the feng shui dream and empower yourself through the energy that is all around you. It is the definitive guide to feng shui, taking you from the very beginning right through to completion. By reading this book you can master:

• The **key concepts** that form the foundation of feng shui (see pages 12–63). Understand these and everything else makes perfect sense. Master what feng shui is and how it works, transforming this fascinating subject from myth and superstition into natural science and something that becomes almost common sense.

• The **different styles of feng shui,** which might sometimes appear to contradict each other. Each school of feng shui is explained (see page 20), so that you can readily identify the various styles and recognize where other attitudes or people are coming from.

• **Chi** (see page 24) – the fundamental 'stuff' on which feng shui is based – a subtle charge of electromagnetic energy that connects your own emotional energy to the space around you. It is the mixing of your own chi with the chi of your home that defines how you feel there.

Deciding what kind of chair to use and where to sit brings all the concepts of feng shui together.

• **Yin and yang** (see page 28) – words that describe the opposing and complementary ways in which you react to the chi that mixes with your own energy field. Yin and yang make the vital connection between you and everything else.

• The **five elements** (wood, fire, soil, metal and water, see page 30) – a remarkable cycle in which five different types of chi interact, thereby bringing solutions to common problems.

• The **five animals** (phoenix, tiger, tortoise, dragon and snake, see page 34), which provide wonderful insights into how simply sitting in a certain part of a room can make you feel better.

• The **eight trigrams** (see page 36), which give character and colour to eight different types of chi. Just by taking in more of one of these energies you can adjust the way you feel and your perception of life.

• The **magic square** (see page 42) – the system that brings everything together and allows you to apply feng shui in all its forms to your home, garden, astrology and yourself.

• The **building blocks of feng shui** (see pages 64–93) – the factors that make a real difference to the feel of a home.

• The **design features** that define the emotional energy of a home (see pages 66–75). Read this section before you redecorate or renovate a building, so that you can make informed choices and design the atmosphere that best suits you.

• **Feng shui remedies** (see pages 78–93) – positive cures that you can employ to enhance the way you feel at home, without having to undertake drastic alterations. These are items that you can buy easily (or may already have) that can be strategically placed to alter the energy around you.

• The processes you need to learn in order to **tailor feng shui in your home to your personal requirements**. Master working with floor plans, making a feng shui map of your home, and reading the way energy flows through each room (see pages 104–123).

• **Applying feng shui to real-life problems**, with suggestions to improve your health (see pages 124–145), moods (see pages 146–169), relationships (see pages 170–197), creativity (see pages 198–225), finances (see pages 226–247), family life (see pages 276–307), career (see pages 308–327) and spirituality (see pages 350–383). The directory also includes special sections on moving home (see pages 248–275) and getting better connected to the natural environment around you (see pages 328–349).

This highly patterned, busy room will be visually stimulating but not ideal for restful sleep.

WHAT IS FENG SHUI?

VITAL ELEMENTS

Feng shui literally translates as 'wind and water'. The mixing, interaction, flow and penetration of these two life-creating elements best describe the essential energy (known as 'chi') that forms the basis of feng shui.

Feng shui is all about understanding the way you interact with your environment. Because your home has one of the biggest influences on your life (and because it is something over which you have control), feng shui tends to focus in practice on people's living spaces. You can of course also apply feng shui to your working environment, your garden, your favourite café or any space where you like to spend time. By understanding the vital connections of feng shui, you can change those things that influence you most and therefore change the way you feel.

The origins of feng shui

Feng shui can be traced back to the ancient civilizations of Egypt, India and China. In fact there are many age-old examples of the basic process of using manmade structures to influence people's feelings -- including stone circles throughout Europe, the great Aztec temples of Central America and the pyramids of Egypt.

Stones were used like aerials to collect and spread energy from the heavens and the earth, to charge up and vitalize an area. Stone circles such as Stonehenge in the UK were designed so that the rising sun's radiation was directed to the centre, intensifying the whole effect. The great pyramids of Egypt and the Aztec temples of Central America used their shape to focus

and combine the earth's natural energies with those coming from space, and to contain it all in their central chambers. Again, openings were employed to encourage sunlight to strike at the heart of a structure.

Pyramids may be one of the earliest examples of people harnessing chi.

Ancient peoples had a great awareness of the solar system and were able to calculate the summer and winter solstices, along with the spring and autumn equinoxes. Built structures were designed so that the sun would concentrate its full force on them during one of these powerful phases.

The Chinese influence

It was in China that the core principles that make up modern feng shui originated. Already embedded in Chinese culture was the concept of how a subtle charge of electromagnetic energy (known as chi) connected people to the world around them; the concepts of yin and yang, the five elements and the trigrams defined how this interaction happened. These concepts were used throughout the Chinese traditions of healing, philosophy, astrology and the martial arts, binding everything together with common threads. Practitioners simply applied the same principles to different subjects.

China is considered the country of origin for feng shui. Part of the challenge of modern feng shui is to put it in a global context.

The philosopher (and later emperor) Fu Hsi is credited with applying the basic concepts to buildings, when he devised his 'magic square' (also known as the 'ba gua'). He can therefore be considered the father of feng shui as we now know it.

How feng shui developed

Like many other ancient worldwide forms of energy manipulation, feng shui was initially applied to burial grounds. Over time its application widened to include important dwellings. In fact it may have been a secret practice, restricted to those in power and not generally available to the masses. During the period of Chinese communism after the Second World War feng shui was suppressed and tended to flourish only in surrounding countries, such as Japan, Hong Kong, Taiwan, Singapore, Malaysia and Korea. Now it has become familiar around the globe.

How feng shui works

Feng shui works on the basis that you have an emotional energy field running through and around your body. The energy can be seen around you as your 'aura'; it flows inside you through activity centres called 'chakras', and out along paths known as 'meridians'. This subtle charge of electromagnetic energy carries your thoughts, ideas and emotions to every cell in your body. It is a two-way process, so the way you use your body also influences your mind and heart, as the altered energy flows back. This process of charging and colouring each cell links your physical and emotional beings.

In addition, your surface energy mixes with the atmosphere around you, with the result that subtle changes occur in the way you think and feel. Over a long period of time this mixing with external energies can even affect your physical body. External influences on your energy fields are many and varied and include: landscapes, cities, the people you live with, homes and workplaces, the weather, the sun's solar energy, the moon and the position of the planets.

Your emotional energy is constantly interacting with the energy of your home – as a result, some of your feelings reflect the place in which you live. Not only that, but your energy spills out into the rooms that you spend time in, filling the atmosphere there with some of your emotions.

To summarize: your thoughts, feelings and ideas constantly mix with the world around you, and you are always being influenced by the different energies entering your own energy field. At the same time you are radiating energy that disperses out into the space you occupy.

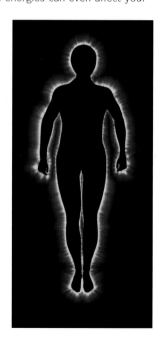

Every living entity is surrounded by an energy field that can be seen using Kirlian photography.

WHAT FENG SHUI CAN DO FOR YOU?

FENG SHUI APPLICATIONS

Experiment and try applying feng shui to your:

• *Health*

• *Moods*

• *Relationships*

• *Creativity*

• *Ability to manage your finances*

• *Family life*

• *Career*

• *Spirituality*

By taking control of the way energy around you mixes with your own energy, you can begin to adjust the way you feel. The aim is to identify what you need to change within yourself so that you are more successful in life. So if you need greater confidence in order to succeed in your career, use feng shui to enhance this characteristic within yourself – rather than assuming that feng shui will somehow make your career more successful.

With this reasoning, you can apply feng shui to any aspect of your life over which you have a direct influence. For example, to make more friends, you might need to become more expressive; to get better results from interviews, you might need to become more assertive; and to enjoy a good relationship with someone, you might need to show greater understanding. What feng shui cannot help with is events that are outside your control. So it is unlikely that money will pour in from nowhere; that the perfect lover will turn up out of the blue; or that the secret of eternal life will suddenly come to you!

Moving home can precipitate long-lasting changes as you live in your new atmosphere.

Is it a feng shui problem?

A major clue to the potential effectiveness of feng shui is whether your problems started after a house move or after making changes to your home. See if you can connect the effect of the move on your emotions with the feng shui of your new home. Another clue is the history of your home. If several of its previous residents suffered similar problems (whether bankruptcy, divorce or ill health), check the feng shui of your home and see if there is an identifiable reason or cause.

Where a move or change has not been made, your home may be of less relevance, but feng shui can still enhance those areas of your life that need attention. Sometimes it only takes a small shift in your own energy to bring about huge changes in your life.

FENG SHUI CHECKLIST

1 Did your problems start after a house move?

2 Have you experienced new difficulties since making changes to your home?

3 Does your house have a history of previous occupiers who experienced similar challenges?

If your answer to any of these question is 'yes', look to see if the feng shui of your home matches the problems you are experiencing.

MYTHS AND SUPERSTITION

Feng shui is based on a set of concepts that are subjective; and like any concept it is not reality itself. Feng shui is simply one way of perceiving the world. The key is not which concepts are right or wrong but which set of concepts or belief system is best for you. If you choose to adopt the feng shui perception of the universe, you will get interesting ideas about how you can better interact with your environment and fresh insights on how to improve your life.

Like many other subjects, feng shui ranges from mere common sense to certain aspects that might stretch even the greatest fan's credulity. To weed out the myths and superstition, it is important to understand the subject and to keep referring back to the key concepts that make sense to you. Anything that you use as a feng shui remedy must change the energy of a space or the way you absorb that energy. For example, a plant radiates its own living energy and therefore changes the energy of a room; turning your bed around exposes you to a different energy while you sleep.

Cultural differences

In Chinese culture, certain objects have a symbolic influence that do not have the same impact on people living outside that culture. For instance, a three-legged toad has specific connotations to some people in China, and each time those people see it, they feel different. Some such objects do not change the atmosphere of a space, but rely on a belief system based on myth and superstition.

MYTH VERSUS REALITY

- **Three-legged toads** Said to bring good luck, but this relies on strong cultural symbolism.

- **Ba gua mirrors** Claimed to reflect negative energy away from a space; but purely in terms of chi flow, a ba gua mirror is similar to any other mirror.

- **Dragons** Used to ward off evil spirits, but these only really work if the recipient believes in them.

- **Pictures of water** Used as a substitute for real water, although they do not change the atmosphere in the way real water does.

- **Flutes** Recommended to move energy upwards, but these objects are grounded in Chinese culture and need a strong belief in order to work.

- **Blessings** Items are blessed by spiritual masters and taken into a space to change its luck; their success depends on the item absorbing another person's chi and radiating this out strongly over a period of time.

- **Silk plants or flowers** Used instead of the real thing, although they do not radiate any living energy.

A ba gua mirror is an eight-sided mirror with the eight trigrams set around a central mirror.

Chinese dragons are said to ward off evil spirits.

THE DIFFERENT SCHOOLS OF FENG SHUI

Because feng shui has developed over thousands of years in so many different locations and civilizations, it is not surprising that different ways of applying it have evolved. Regardless of the system, the key concepts of chi, yin and yang, the five elements, the trigrams and the magic square remain the same, although the method used to analyse and create solutions varies. There are five schools in common use and they are described below. They all use Chinese feng shui as their source, although one school was developed in New York and another in Japan. It is thought that feng shui started six thousand years ago, although it is hard to discern exactly when the various styles originated. It is likely that they evolved slowly over long periods of time as society and civilization developed.

Compass and non-compass schools

One essential difference is that in more mountainous areas of China, the landscape was considered to be the greatest influence on setting up a home, whereas on the plains the sun was the predominant force. Buildings that were orientated on the position of the sun catalysed a feng shui system based on taking compass readings, whereas non-compass feng shui used the surrounding landscape to orientate the different chi energies.

Form school

In this school, the shapes and forms of the landscape are studied to try and identify four mystical animals: the phoenix, tiger, tortoise and dragon. These are then used to map out the natural flow of chi through the terrain, in a way that helps orientate and set up a dwelling. The idea is that the front

consists of a big open vista (represented by the phoenix), while mountains, trees or hills protect the

This dramatic landscape can conjure up the imagery of the Chinese animals used to help orientate a new building.

rear (symbolized by the tortoise). On the right there should be some form of low, solid protection (represented by the tiger) and on the left a lighter, taller structure (the dragon).

Three-gate school

This is a relatively new style of feng shui, developed during the 1970s in New York. The position of the door to a building or room orientates the magic square (ba gua), which is placed over the floor plan, creating a map of how the chi will flow in the house and in each room. Each sector of the ba gua represents an area of your life: the far left corner = wealth; far centre = fame; far right = relationships; mid-right = children; near right = helpful people; near centre = career; near left = knowledge; mid-left = family; centre = yourself.

Eight mansions school

In this Chinese compass-based approach, your date of birth defines your kua number (the chi you were born with) and whether you are part of a west- or east-life group. From this, homes facing four of the eight compass directions are favourable to you, while homes facing the other four directions can be negative. In addition, half your home is generally positive to you and the other half potentially harmful. Your life group, the direction in which the building faces and the position of your main entrance define which half is which.

Flying star school

In this traditional Chinese compass-based system, an astrology chart of the period in which your building was constructed is merged with a chart of the present year, and the magic square is then orientated according to the layout of the building and its surroundings. For this method a special compass called a 'lo pan' is used to take readings. It consists of a compass set in

A Lo Pan compass carries useful information on the position of various energies.

a disc with concentric circles giving feng shui information. The disc sits in a square box, with two red cords bisecting the centre of the compass. The box can be held against a wall to take readings. The feng shui of the building needs to be updated each year as the new year's chart takes effect.

Eight directions school

This is a Japanese development of the traditional Chinese compass-based feng shui. In this school, a compass is used to orientate the eight directions over your home's floor plan. Based on the magic square, each direction carries a specific kind of energy into the home. This can either be enhanced or calmed, according to your needs. In addition, your sleeping and sitting positions determine which of the energies you absorb more of. Rather than the energies being seen as positive or negative, they are simply used to enhance your energy field in a way that makes you feel happier.

Combinations of styles

The eight mansions and flying star systems are often used together, and sometimes the form school is also included. None of the styles can be said to be better or more effective than any other, so it really comes down to which system you feel makes most sense, is most applicable and inspires you. In this book you will learn how to use the eight directions school of feng shui. This is relatively easy to learn and encompasses all the principles of feng shui in a way that is simple to understand. Combined with this is the nine ki feng shui astrology system (see page 36), which uses the same principles to add a time dimension to the space on which feng shui focuses.

CHI

Chi is the subtle charge of electromagnetic energy that runs through everything, carrying information from one thing to another. The chi flowing through your body predominantly carries your thoughts, beliefs and emotions.

Sitting in this window will expose you to strong currents of chi making it a stimulating place to think.

All the time some of your chi is floating off, while you are also drawing in new energy. The fresh chi that you draw into your own energy field brings with it something of the world around you. This includes the energy of the weather, the chi of other people, the atmosphere of your home and the living energy of the food you eat. As this chi enters your energy field, it alters your own chi, resulting in you feeling different and having new thoughts.

Your energy field connects you to everything else, whether you like it or not. The secret to making this energy work is understanding the process and finding out how you can make it help you in life.

Chi in your home

Different areas of your home contain different quantities and qualities of chi:
• There are particularly strong currents of chi around doors and windows. Where there are several doors in a straight line, this can lead to a fast flow of chi, making the home hard to relax in.

- The larger your home's windows, the faster chi can flow, making for an active space. Windows that face a sunny direction bring in livelier, more fiery and stimulating chi.

- The chi moving through doors and windows generates a horizontal flow, especially if the ceilings are low. This is common in apartments situated close to ground level. The effect of this horizontal flow is that chi passes readily from one person to the next, making the space ideal for social and interactive gatherings.

- Spaces that have high ceilings or that are set on the side of a hill or at the top of a building have a more vertical flow of chi. This is typical in loft apartments and spaces with a pointed ceiling. It is easier to feel more individualistic here, to come up with original ideas and dare to be different.

- Sharp corners pointing into a room generate a strong flow of piercing chi. If a corner points towards your bed or chair, you may find it hard to sleep well or settle there.

- The people who live in a house also influence its atmosphere. Arguments, unhappiness or violence can fill a room with negative chi and, over a period of time, the space may begin to carry that atmosphere.

This low sloping ceiling compresses chi making it harder to think freely while sitting below it.

YOUR CHAKRAS, MERIDIANS AND AURA

In the human body there is a strong current of chi energy that spirals into a main central channel through the top of your head. As energy moves through the body, it forms seven strong energy centres, where it swirls around. These activity centres are known as chakras; they are important places for changing the flow of chi throughout your body.

If you look at the top of a baby's head (or someone with very short hair) you will see a spiral. This is the crown chakra, where environmental energy most easily enters the body. While you sleep you are in a more receptive state, so it is then that you generally recharge your chi. In feng shui it is very important to notice which way the top of your head points while you sleep, as this determines the kind of energy that you absorb.

From your chakras run large channels of energy, known as meridians; rather like main blood vessels, they feed energy to the rest of your torso, arms and legs. Along each meridian are points where you can change the energy more easily – these are known as acupressure points, or 'tsubos'. You can change the energy here by massaging them with your fingers (acupressure), by heating them (moxibustion) or by carefully pushing a fine metal needle into them (acupuncture).

You also have an outer energy field that makes up your aura. This is where you interact most easily with the world around you, and it is sometimes called your 'sixth sense'. At times you can project this energy out further (rather like an antenna), reaching out into the world around you to tap into the vast array of cosmic information. Your ability to do this can provide you with intuitive insights and amazing new ideas.

DISCOVERING THE CHI OF THE CHAKRAS

To locate someone's chakras, you need to tie a cotton thread about 1 m (3 ft) long around a metal ring, so that you can suspend the ring. Get your friend to lie down, then slowly move the ring over his or her body to see if you can find areas of more intense, spiralling chi.

When you find a chakra, the ring should begin to circle on the end of its thread. The direction in which it circles reflects the way the energy spirals – rather like the vortex created by water as it drains from a bath.

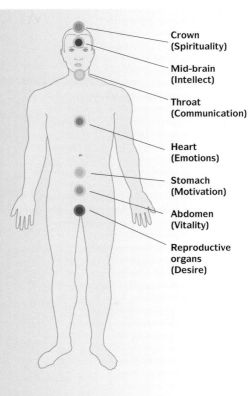

Crown
(Spirituality)

Mid-brain
(Intellect)

Throat
(Communication)

Heart
(Emotions)

Stomach
(Motivation)

Abdomen
(Vitality)

Reproductive
organs
(Desire)

The chi in each of the seven chakras relates to a different aspect of your character.

YIN AND YANG

'Yin' and 'yang' are words used to describe different forms
of chi. Yin chi is slower, more dispersed and cooler. Yang
chi is faster, more compressed and hotter. Literally, they
mean the shady side of the mountain (yin) and the sunny side
(yang). They are complementary and opposing forms that allow you to connect
yourself to everything around you; in this way, you can quickly decide what you
need to do to bring yourself back into balance.

People are always more yin or more yang, and most of the time this is
healthy. But sometimes you may experience problems from being too yin or
too yang, so, once you have identified which you are, simply take in more of
the opposite type of chi and reduce the one of which you have an excess.

The boxes opposite show how this works. For example, if you find
something in the 'too yin' list that affects you, try ideas from the list entitled 'to
become more yang' and reduce those in the list entitled 'to become more yin'.

Natural yin qualities

Look for an oval-shaped face, a lean frame and long fingers and toes. Large
eyes, full lips and fleshy cheeks are also more yin. Someone who blinks often
and finds it hard to make eye contact will be more yin.

Yin qualities include being creative, imaginative, sensitive, flexible, easy-
going and gentle. However, anyone who is naturally more yin can slip into
becoming too yin more easily than becoming too yang.

Natural yang qualities

A rounder face, stockier build and solid look are more yang. Small eyes, thin
lips and a well-developed jawline emphasize the point.

Yang qualities include being focused, alert, precise, active and thriving on a dynamic lifestyle. It is easier for such people to be too yang than to go through periods of being yin.

TOO YIN

- *Feeling cold*
- *Frequent infectious illnesses*
- *Cold, clammy skin*
- *Diarrhoea*
- *Lethargy*
- *Depression*
- *Victim mentality*

TOO YANG

- *Stiffness/tightness*
- *Tension*
- *Dry skin*
- *Constipation*
- *Stress*
- *Anger*
- *A need to be in control*

TO BECOME MORE YIN

- *Meditate*
- *Eat more fresh fruit and salads*
- *Drink water and juices*
- *Wear clothes in pastel colours*
- *Wear loose, flowing clothes*
- *Try stretching exercises*
- *Get out into nature*
- *Listen to relaxing music*
- *Use soft lighting or candles*

TO BECOME MORE YANG

- *Do martial arts*
- *Play competitive sports*
- *Wear bright colours*
- *Dress up in smart, formal clothes*
- *Socialize*
- *Eat cooked foods*
- *Eat more root vegetables, grains and fish*
- *Get rid of clutter*
- *Exercise*

THE FIVE ELEMENTS

The five elements define how chi energies interact with each other – they comprise a model in which energies can feed, calm or destroy each other. Each of the five types of chi is similar to an atmosphere that you might experience at a certain time of day and in a particular season. They are named after elements found in nature: wood, fire, soil, metal and water.

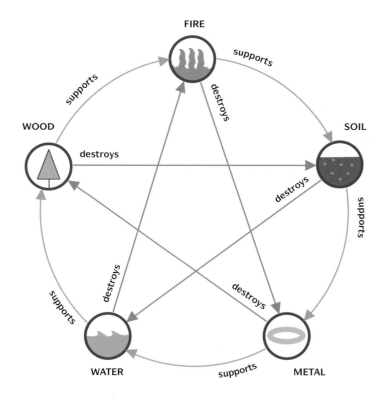

*Looking out at the sun setting on the horizon in September
enables you to experience the feeling of metal chi.*

ELEMENT ATTRIBUTES

- **Wood** *energy is upward, active and full of new hopes – just like you might feel
on a sunny spring morning. It represents the rising sun in the east.*

- **Fire** *is outward, expressive and colourful – similar to the middle of a hot
summer's day. This is the midday sun in the south.*

- **Soil** *resembles the downward, settled and secure energy of the descending
south-western sun. It symbolizes the end of the summer in the afternoon.*

- **Metal** *describes chi moving inwards, becoming concentrated and contained –
like watching a big autumn sunset in the west with a sense of completion.*

- **Water** *relates to going with the flow, being flexible and regenerating deeply –
imagine the middle of the night in midwinter, facing north.*

*If you live in the Southern Hemisphere, swap north and south in the decriptions
above but leave east and west in place.*

THE FIVE ELEMENTS IN ACTION

Here are some practical examples of the ways that you can apply the five elements to your life:

Feeling withdrawn, lonely or unnoticed? *See if you have a toilet, sink, bath, shower or washing machine (water) in the south (fire) part of your home, and whether there is a lack of wood chi. Tip: water destroys fire without wood. To complete the five-element cycle, put more wood chi in the room, in the form of plants, wooden flooring, furniture or objects, or use the colour green.*

Cannot feel romantic or content, or put money in the bank? *Check to see if you have a fireplace, stove, boiler or oven (fire) in the west (metal) part of your home. Tip: fire destroys metal without soil. Put more soil energy there, in the form of charcoal in a clay pot, yellow flowers in a clay container, a soft stone floor, or use the colour yellow.*

Feeling isolated, quiet and like hiding away? *Check to see if your bathroom (water) or other water features are in the north (water). Tip: too much water chi; calm the water chi with wood chi, and restrict the metal chi. Grow lots of plants (wood) in your bathroom and take away any metal objects.*

When all of these energies are present, they work in perfect harmony, feeding and calming each other. Look at the chart and you will see that water feeds wood, wood feeds fire, and so on. At the same time, wood calms water, fire calms wood, and so on around the circle. For example, too much fire chi is calmed by less wood and more soil; too little fire chi is increased by more wood and less soil.

When one of the five elements is seriously deficient, the preceding energy can destroy the following energy. For instance, if fire chi is seriously deficient, then wood chi energy would be destructive to soil chi.

The most common situations where two types of chi energy enter into a destructive relationship are where fire or water is concerned. In the home, this means boilers, fireplaces, stoves and ovens for fire energy, and bathrooms, toilets, kitchen sinks, washing machines and dishwashers for water energy. The remedy is simply to add more of the deficient energy. So in a bathroom in the south part of your home, you would need to add more wood energy to restore a harmonious relationship between water, wood and fire.

Plants will absorb water chi from the sink, helping to subdue the water chi if it is not harmonious with the ambient chi.

THE FIVE ANIMALS

The five animals – the dragon, phoenix, tiger, tortoise and snake – represent your outer energy field. Your natural flow of chi will be more powerful if you are sitting or standing in the right position when it merges naturally with the surrounding chi.

The five animals provide the imagery of the type of chi around your body. This chi external field moves with you – the phoenix is always in front of you.

The chi in front of you (the phoenix) spreads out and rises, so it will be free to do this if you have a large, open space before you. To your right your chi is represented by the tiger, whose aim is to guard and move forward with you (the arm of a chair, a solid squat item of furniture or a low wall could achieve this). Your rear is protected by the symbolic hard shell of the tortoise, and this chi seeks solid structures (the back of a chair, a wall, tree or mountain). The dragon flies to your left, seeking new opportunities, so this chi could be nourished by anything that has a lighter feel (such as a light table, fountain or hedge). The snake sits in the centre of the four animals and represents you.

The ideal place to sit

Where the concept of the five animals is particularly useful is in choosing somewhere to sit – whether it is at home, in a café or restaurant, at work or in meetings. Armed with this knowledge, you will be able to find the most powerful position to support your chi. The aim is to ensure that you have as much of the room as possible in front of you, and preferably a good view of the entrance and windows – this means that the phoenix will be free to expand and fill the space before you. Equally important is to find a wall, a high-backed chair or some tall furniture to protect your back; it is very distracting and leaves you in a weak position if you have your back to an area where there is plenty of activity (for example, a busy doorway). If possible, have something solid and low to your right (a chest or heavy table) and something lighter to your left (a plant or lamp stand).

NINE NUMBERS

The principle of the nine numbers is that you are surrounded by eight different kinds of chi, so by turning to a new direction you face a different type of chi. The chi is different because of the way the sun affects the planet, the earth's magnetic field and the forces of other planets. This means that you can absorb more of one particular type of chi into your own energy field and take on more of the characteristics of that energy. The easiest way to do this is to sleep so that the top of your head points in the direction representing the energy that you think you need more of.

In this system the nine energies are divided into the four points of the compass (north, east, south and west), the four directions in between (north-east, north-west, south-east and south-west) and one for the centre. Each type of chi is given a number from one to nine, which refers to the energy's position in the magic square (ba gua). To clarify the energy of each direction, it is associated with a time of day, a season, an element and a trigram. (A trigram is a series of three parallel lines, which are either solid or broken; the solid lines are yang and the broken lines are yin.) The trigrams are linked to a family member (such as the eldest son), and those that have one of the five elements in common have their own unique symbol from nature (such as thunder).

Read through the description given on pages 37–41 for each direction to see if you need more of any particular type of chi.

Each direction is associated with a certain character of chi. Understanding the different flavours of chi is essential to mastering feng shui.

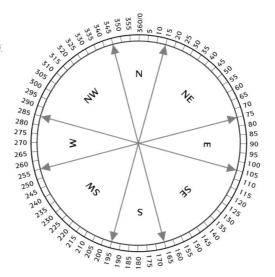

EAST

Magic-square number 3	**Trigram** Yin/yin/yang
Element Wood	**Symbol** Thunder
Family member Eldest son	**Colour** Bright green, similar to a new leaf
Time Morning – sunrise	**Season** Spring

Helpful for feeling enthusiastic, confident and assertive; strengthens the desire to start new projects, be alert, focus on details, get things right, analyse, be precise and concentrate. The symbol of thunder gives this energy a loud, forceful edge, encouraging you to go out and make things happen. This chi is useful if you want to wake and get up early, but it can increase the risk of experiencing frustration and anger.

SOUTH-EAST

Magic-square number 4

Trigram Yang/yang/yin

Element Wood

Symbol Wind

Family member Eldest daughter

Colour The same dark green as a mature leaf; a sky-blue

Time Mid-morning – sun rising in the sky

Season Spring changing to summer

Helpful for being persistent, sensitive and positive; increases the desire to be creative and imaginative, to generate new ideas, seek harmony and communicate. It is ideal for spreading ideas, rather as the wind spreads seeds. This chi is good for making progress in life and working on future prosperity, but it can increase the risk of feeling irritable and impatient.

SOUTH

Magic-square number 9

Trigram Yang/yin/yang

Element Fire

Symbol Fire

Family member Middle daughter

Colour A fiery bright reddish-purple

Time Midday – the sun at its highest point

Season Midsummer

Good for feeling passionate, excited, proud, generous, flamboyant and dramatic; but can also lead to feeling self-centred, stressed and hysterical. It increases the desire to be expressive, get noticed, be sociable, outgoing and spontaneous, lead fashions and be quick-minded. This fiery energy is bright, colourful and radiates chi. The risk is that you could feel stressed, over-emotional and suffer from hysteria.

SOUTH-WEST

Magic-square number 2

Element Soil

Family member Mother

Trigram Yin/yin/yin

Symbol Earth

Colour Matt black, brown, beige or yellow; similar to charcoal or soil

Time Afternoon – sun moving down in the sky

Season Summer changing to autumn

Good for being caring, patient and sympathetic; increases the desire to be practical and down-to-earth, to consolidate and be secure. It is the ideal chi for improving the quality of whatever you do. Think of fruits ripening on the vine. This settling-soil chi is helpful for deepening all kinds of relationships. However, it can increase the risk of feeling dependent and jealous.

WEST

Magic-square number 7

Element Metal

Family member Youngest daughter

Trigram Yin/yang/yang

Symbol Lake

Colour The colour of the sunset; rusty-red, maroon or pink

Time Early evening – sunset

Season Autumn

Good for feeling romantic, content and playful; increases the desire to be wealthy, form new relationships, be stylish and complete projects. Associated with harvest time and the end of the day, this chi is ideal for bringing things to a profitable conclusion. The youngest-daughter chi is associated with being playful, seeking fun and enjoying the pleasures of life, but it can increase the risk of feeling depressed and pessimistic.

NORTH-WEST

Magic-square number 6	**Trigram** Yang/yang/yang
Element Metal	**Symbol** Heaven
Family member Father	**Colour** Silver-grey or off-white; close to the colour of metal
Time Late evening – dusk	**Season** Autumn changing to winter

Good for being in charge, dignified and responsible; increases the desire to feel in control, organize, plan ahead, be respected and have integrity. The symbol of heaven means that this chi is helpful for greater wisdom and clearer intuition; it represents experience and maturity, and finding it easy to win people's trust, command respect or find a mentor. However, it can increase the risk of being authoritarian and arrogant.

NORTH

Magic-square number 1	**Trigram** Yin/yang/yin
Element Water	**Symbol** Water
Family member Middle son	**Colour** Cream with a high gloss finish, clear varnish or other translucent finish; glossy black
Time Night – darkness	**Season** Midwinter

Good for feeling sexual, spiritual and independent; increases the desire to be flexible, find peace, study, develop yourself, improve health, be objective and different. This chi is useful for getting original ideas without being distracted by others; it is ideal for conception, healing yourself and vitality. This quiet chi is also helpful if you have trouble sleeping, but there is a risk of feeling isolated and aloof.

NORTH-EAST

Magic-square number 8

Trigram ☶ Yang/yin/yin

Element Soil

Symbol Mountain

Family member Youngest son

Colour A brilliant white, rather like a snow-peaked mountain

Time Early morning – the first haze of light

Season Winter changing to spring

Good for being motivated, driven and outgoing; increases the desire to seize opportunities, win, compete, learn, be decisive, clear-minded and adventurous. This chi is sharp, piercing and quick to change, making it good for striking a deal and trading. It is also useful for clearing your mind, helping to be more decisive and thinking of a new direction in life. However, it can also encourage you to be greedy and obsessive.

CENTRE

Magic-square number 5

Trigram None

Element Soil

Symbol None

Family member None

Colour Yellow or orange

Time None

Season None

This energy links all the eight directions. It does not have a specific trigram, time or season, but can be said to represent them all. As such, it is an energy that can help you become the centre of attention and attract people to you. It is the most powerful of all the chi and is therefore treated with respect. If possible, the centre of a room or building should be kept clear and open to allow this energy room to move.

THE MAGIC SQUARE

The one thing that binds all the feng shui concepts together is the magic square. This is a grid of nine numbers, where each number represents one of the energies from the eight directions, along with the centre. The numbers are arranged so that whichever way you add them up – horizontally, vertically or diagonally – they always total 15.

When applied to a home, the magic square is arranged in its standard form, with the number 5 in the centre. However, it can also be arranged so that each of the other eight numbers takes a turn in the centre, with the surrounding numbers adjusted accordingly. The ability of the square to transform through nine phases enables you to apply it to both time and space, in the form of feng shui astrology and the feng shui of your home.

4	9	2
3	5	7
8	1	6

The Magic Square

When the numbers are arranged in their standard form 1 is aligned with the north. The numbers then follow the compass in a clockwise direction, so that 8 is in the north-east, 3 in the east, 4 in the south-east, 9 in the south, 2 in the south-west, 7 in the west, 6 in the north-west, along with 5 in the centre.

In this nine ki system (named after 'ki', the Japanese word for chi), the north, east, south and west portions each take up 30 degrees, with the remaining directions in between (north-east, south-east, south-west and north-west) each taking up 60 degrees (see page 113).

It is important not to confuse the nine ki numbers with numbers in everyday life: house numbers, phone numbers, and so on. The nine numbers used here are names for the chi they represent, and it essential to keep the character of the chi in mind when referring to these numbers.

The nine patterns of chi

Each chart below represents one of the nine patterns of chi. Using these nine charts, you can work out which phase you are in, which directions are best for you, and the right time to carry out work in your home.

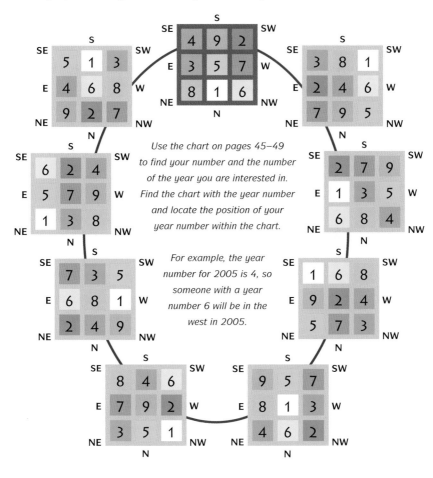

Use the chart on pages 45–49 to find your number and the number of the year you are interested in. Find the chart with the year number and locate the position of your year number within the chart.

For example, the year number for 2005 is 4, so someone with a year number 6 will be in the west in 2005.

FIND YOUR OWN NUMBERS FROM THE MAGIC SQUARE

In the nine ki system used here, each person has three numbers from the magic square, and each number connects you with the chi corresponding to that number (see page 36). The three numbers make up your year, month and axis number. The year number defines your deepest chi, which moves through your chakras; the month number describes the chi of your heart and mind; and your axis number illustrates your superficial chi.

Using the nine ki chart

To find your three numbers, use the chart to locate the year and month in which you were born. The nine ki system uses a solar calendar, so the years and months do not begin at the same time as ours. The nine ki year starts on 3, 4 or 5 February. Each month in the chart has a date and time to indicate when the nine ki month starts. If you were born before this date, you need to refer to the previous month. For instance, if you were born on 2 August 1958, you use the numbers for July 1958: 692.

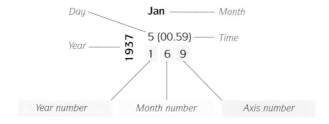

	Jan	Feb	March	April	May	June	July	Aug	Sept	Oct	Nov	Dec
1937	5 (00:59)	4 (14:30)	6 (10:34)	4 (17:32)	5 (13:20)	5 (19:34)	7 (08:41)	7 (19:57)	8 (00:37)	8 (18:13)	7 (23:00)	7 (17:30)
	1 6 9	9 5 9	9 4 1	9 3 2	9 2 3	9 1 4	9 9 5	9 8 6	9 7 7	9 6 8	9 5 9	9 4 1
1938	6 (06:40)	4 (20:23)	6 (16:22)	4 (23:12)	5 (18:51)	6 (01:01)	7 (14:08)	8 (01:28)	8 (06:13)	8 (23:57)	8 (04:53)	7 (23:29)
	9 3 2	8 2 2	8 1 3	8 9 4	8 8 5	8 7 6	8 6 7	8 5 8	8 4 9	8 3 1	8 2 2	8 1 3
1939	6 (12:41)	5 (02:08)	6 (22:13)	5 (05:24)	6 (00:24)	6 (07:39)	7 (19:37)	8 (07:02)	8 (12:45)	9 (05:46)	8 (10:48)	8 (05:28)
	8 9 4	7 8 4	7 7 5	7 6 6	7 5 7	7 4 8	7 3 9	7 2 1	7 1 2	7 9 3	7 8 4	7 7 5
1940	6 (18:43)	5 (08:09)	6 (04:15)	4 (11:13)	5 (07:00)	5 (13:15)	7 (01:09)	7 (13:42)	8 (18:20)	8 (11:25)	7 (16:33)	7 (11:12)
	7 6 6	6 5 6	6 4 7	6 3 8	6 2 9	6 1 1	6 9 2	6 8 3	6 7 4	6 6 5	6 5 6	6 4 7
1941	6 (00:07)	4 (13:54)	6 (10:00)	4 (16:56)	5 (12:40)	5 (18:52)	7 (08:00)	7 (19:19)	8 (00:02)	8 (17:40)	7 (22:29)	6 (17:17)
	6 3 8	5 2 8	5 1 9	5 9 1	5 8 2	5 7 3	5 6 4	5 5 5	5 4 6	5 3 7	5 2 8	5 1 9
1942	6 (06:10)	4 (19:55)	6 (15:57)	4 (22:47)	5 (18:24)	6 (00:29)	7 (13:31)	8 (00:48)	8 (05:33)	8 (23:18)	8 (04:16)	7 (22:53)
	5 9 1	4 8 1	4 7 2	4 6 3	4 5 4	4 4 5	4 3 6	4 2 7	4 1 8	4 9 9	4 8 1	4 7 2
1943	6 (12:08)	5 (01:38)	6 (21:46)	5 (04:58)	5 (23:58)	6 (07:08)	7 (18:59)	8 (06:20)	8 (12:00)	9 (05:00)	8 (10:02)	8 (04:43)
	4 6 3	3 5 3	3 4 4	3 3 5	3 2 6	3 1 7	3 9 8	3 8 9	3 7 1	3 6 2	3 5 3	3 4 4
1944	6 (17:57)	5 (07:24)	6 (03:32)	4 (10:33)	5 (06:25)	5 (12:43)	7 (00:38)	7 (13:10)	7 (17:48)	8 (10:52)	7 (16:00)	7 (10:41)
	3 3 5	2 2 5	2 1 6	2 9 7	2 8 8	2 7 9	2 6 1	2 5 2	2 4 3	2 3 4	2 2 5	2 1 6
1945	5 (23:37)	4 (13:23)	6 (09:28)	4 (16:24)	5 (12:08)	5 (18:21)	7 (07:25)	7 (18:41)	7 (23:19)	8 (16:52)	7 (21:40)	7 (16:25)
	2 9 7	1 8 7	1 7 8	1 6 9	1 5 1	1 4 2	1 3 3	1 2 4	1 1 5	1 9 6	1 8 7	1 7 8
1946	6 (05:24)	4 (19:11)	6 (15:13)	4 (22:04)	5 (17:40)	5 (23:47)	7 (12:52)	8 (00:11)	8 (04:56)	8 (22:38)	8 (03:32)	7 (22:06)
	1 6 9	9 5 9	9 4 1	9 3 2	9 2 3	9 1 4	9 9 5	9 8 6	9 7 7	9 6 8	9 5 9	9 4 1
1947	6 (11:19)	5 (00:48)	6 (20:55)	5 (04:08)	5 (23:09)	6 (06:23)	7 (18:18)	8 (05:43)	8 (11:27)	9 (04:28)	8 (09:29)	8 (04:06)
	9 3 2	8 2 2	8 1 3	8 9 4	8 8 5	8 7 6	8 6 7	8 5 8	8 4 9	8 3 1	8 2 2	8 1 3
1948	6 (17:18)	5 (06:43)	6 (02:50)	4 (09:50)	5 (05:39)	5 (11:55)	6 (23:49)	7 (12:21)	7 (16:59)	8 (10:05)	7 (15:13)	7 (09:51)
	8 9 4	7 8 4	7 7 5	7 6 6	7 5 7	7 4 8	7 3 9	7 2 1	7 1 2	7 9 3	7 8 4	7 7 5
1949	5 (22:43)	4 (12:26)	6 (08:30)	4 (15:25)	5 (11:11)	5 (17:25)	7 (05:18)	7 (17:52)	7 (22:36)	8 (16:15)	7 (21:05)	7 (15:50)
	7 6 6	6 5 6	6 4 7	6 3 8	6 2 9	6 1 1	6 9 2	6 8 3	6 7 4	6 6 5	6 5 6	6 4 7
1950	6 (04:46)	4 (18:27)	6 (14:24)	4 (21:10)	5 (16:46)	5 (22:52)	7 (11:57)	7 (23:17)	8 (04:04)	8 (21:49)	8 (02:49)	7 (21:28)
	6 3 8	5 2 8	5 1 9	5 9 1	5 8 2	5 7 3	5 6 4	5 5 5	5 4 6	5 3 7	5 2 8	5 1 9
1951	6 (10:43)	5 (00:11)	6 (20:15)	5 (03:21)	5 (22:18)	6 (05:27)	7 (17:20)	8 (04:43)	8 (09:36)	9 (03:28)	8 (08:31)	8 (03:11)
	5 9 1	4 8 1	4 7 2	4 6 3	4 5 4	4 4 5	4 3 6	4 2 7	4 1 8	4 9 9	4 8 1	4 7 2
1952	6 (16:26)	5 (05:53)	6 (01:59)	4 (08:56)	5 (04:43)	5 (10:58)	6 (22:52)	7 (11:28)	7 (16:09)	8 (09:17)	7 (14:25)	7 (09:08)
	4 6 3	3 5 3	3 4 4	3 3 5	3 2 6	3 1 7	3 9 8	3 8 9	3 7 1	3 6 2	3 5 3	3 4 4
1953	5 (22:04)	4 (11:49)	6 (07:53)	4 (14:46)	5 (10:28)	6 (16:36)	7 (04:25)	7 (16:55)	7 (21:37)	8 (15:15)	7 (20:07)	7 (14:53)
	3 3 5	2 2 5	2 1 6	2 9 7	2 8 8	2 7 9	2 6 1	2 5 2	2 4 3	2 3 4	2 2 5	2 1 6

Find your own numbers from the magic square

Feng shui basics

Year		Jan	Feb	March	April	May	June	July	Aug	Sept	Oct	Nov	Dec
1954		6 (03:52)	4 (17:37)	6 (13:38)	4 (20:27)	5 (16:01)	5 (22:05)	7 (11:06)	7 (22:24)	8 (03:10)	8 (20:56)	8 (01:55)	7 (20:33)
		2 9 7	1 8 7	1 7 8	1 6 9	1 5 1	1 4 2	1 3 3	1 2 4	1 1 5	1 9 6	1 8 7	1 7 8
1955		6 (09:47)	4 (23:14)	6 (19:18)	5 (02:29)	5 (21:28)	6 (03:30)	7 (16:34)	8 (03:58)	8 (08:51)	9 (02:44)	8 (07:50)	8 (02:31)
		1 6 9	9 5 9	9 4 1	9 3 2	9 2 3	9 1 4	9 9 5	9 8 6	9 7 7	9 6 8	9 5 9	9 4 1
1956		6 (15:46)	5 (05:11)	6 (01:17)	4 (00:14)	5 (04:00)	5 (10:16)	6 (22:08)	7 (10:39)	7 (12:15)	8 (08:22)	7 (13:30)	7 (08:14)
		9 3 2	8 2 2	8 1 3	8 9 4	8 8 5	8 7 6	8 6 7	8 5 8	8 4 9	8 3 1	8 2 2	8 1 3
1957		5 (21:12)	4 (10:57)	6 (07:01)	4 (13:54)	5 (09:36)	5 (15:47)	7 (03:40)	7 (16:14)	7 (20:57)	8 (14:35)	7 (19:26)	7 (14:11)
		8 9 4	7 8 4	7 7 5	7 6 6	7 5 7	7 4 8	7 3 9	7 2 1	7 1 2	7 9 3	7 8 4	7 7 5
1958		6 (03:10)	4 (16:54)	6 (09:43)	4 (19:40)	5 (15:14)	5 (21:18)	7 (10:22)	7 (21:43)	8 (02:32)	8 (20:19)	8 (01:17)	7 (19:54)
		7 6 6	6 5 6	6 4 7	6 3 8	6 2 9	6 1 1	6 9 2	6 8 3	6 7 4	6 6 5	6 5 6	6 4 7
1959		6 (09:09)	2 (22:48)	6 (18:45)	5 (01:54)	5 (20:51)	6 (02:50)	7 (15:51)	8 (03:14)	8 (08:09)	9 (02:03)	8 (07:07)	8 (01:45)
		6 3 8	5 2 8	5 1 9	5 9 1	5 8 2	5 7 3	5 6 4	5 5 5	5 4 6	5 3 7	5 2 8	5 1 9
1960		6 (14:58)	5 (04:23)	6 (00:29)	4 (07:27)	5 (03:15)	5 (09:30)	6 (21:25)	7 (10:01)	7 (14:44)	8 (07:55)	7 (13:05)	7 (07:49)
		5 9 1	4 8 1	4 7 2	4 6 3	4 5 4	4 4 5	4 3 6	4 2 7	4 1 8	4 9 9	4 8 1	4 7 2
1961		5 (20:43)	4 (10:25)	6 (06:25)	4 (13:18)	5 (09:00)	5 (15:11)	7 (03:01)	7 (15:33)	7 (20:16)	8 (13:57)	7 (18:52)	7 (13:41)
		4 6 3	3 5 3	3 4 4	3 3 5	3 2 6	3 1 7	3 9 8	3 8 9	3 7 1	3 6 2	3 5 3	3 4 4
1962		6 (02:41)	4 (16:23)	6 (12:19)	4 (19:03)	5 (14:36)	5 (20:40)	7 (09:42)	7 (21:02)	8 (01:50)	8 (19:38)	8 (00:40)	7 (19:21)
		3 3 5	2 2 5	2 1 6	2 9 7	2 8 8	2 7 9	2 6 1	2 5 2	2 4 3	2 3 4	2 2 5	2 1 6
1963		6 (08:37)	4 (22:04)	6 (18:05)	5 (01:10)	5 (20:05)	6 (02:06)	7 (15:10)	8 (02:37)	8 (07:34)	9 (01:30)	8 (06:37)	8 (01:21)
		2 9 7	1 8 7	1 7 8	1 6 9	1 5 1	1 4 2	1 3 3	1 2 4	1 1 5	1 9 6	1 8 7	1 7 8
1964		6 (14:38)	5 (04:04)	6 (00:08)	4 (07:02)	5 (01:51)	5 (08:55)	6 (20:47)	7 (09:19)	7 (15:25)	8 (07:09)	7 (12:19)	7 (07:05)
		1 6 9	9 5 9	9 4 1	9 3 2	9 2 3	9 1 4	9 9 5	9 8 6	9 7 7	9 6 8	9 5 9	9 4 1
1965		5 (20:02)	4 (09:48)	6 (05:52)	4 (12:44)	5 (08:22)	5 (14:29)	7 (02:18)	7 (14:51)	7 (19:36)	8 (13:18)	7 (18:12)	7 (13:00)
		9 3 2	8 2 2	8 1 3	8 9 4	8 8 5	8 7 6	8 6 7	8 5 8	8 4 9	8 3 1	8 2 2	8 1 3
1966		6 (01:59)	4 (15:42)	6 (11:41)	4 (18:26)	5 (13:58)	5 (20:00)	7 (09:00)	7 (20:19)	8 (01:08)	8 (18:58)	8 (00:00)	7 (18:42)
		8 9 4	7 8 4	7 7 5	7 6 6	7 5 7	7 4 8	7 3 9	7 2 1	7 1 2	7 9 3	7 8 4	7 7 5
1967		6 (07:58)	4 (21:26)	6 (17:30)	5 (00:07)	5 (19:33)	6 (01:30)	7 (14:29)	8 (01:49)	8 (06:42)	9 (00:36)	8 (05:42)	8 (00:25)
		7 6 6	6 5 6	6 4 7	6 3 8	6 2 9	6 1 1	6 9 2	6 8 3	6 7 4	6 6 5	6 5 6	6 4 7
1968		6 (13:41)	5 (03:06)	5 (23:11)	4 (06:06)	5 (00:58)	5 (08:05)	6 (19:59)	7 (07:24)	7 (13:13)	8 (06:22)	7 (11:33)	7 (06:19)
		6 3 8	5 2 8	5 1 9	5 9 1	5 8 2	5 7 3	5 6 4	5 5 5	5 4 6	5 3 7	5 2 8	5 1 9
1969		5 (19:16)	4 (09:00)	6 (05:02)	4 (11:53)	5 (07:32)	5 (13:41)	7 (01:30)	7 (14:03)	7 (18:45)	8 (11:59)	7 (17:17)	7 (12:06)
		5 9 1	4 8 1	4 7 2	4 6 3	4 5 4	4 4 5	4 3 6	4 2 7	4 1 8	4 9 9	4 8 1	4 7 2
1970		6 (01:21)	4 (14:51)	6 (10:48)	4 (17:33)	5 (13:04)	5 (19:06)	7 (08:07)	7 (19:27)	8 (00:16)	8 (18:03)	7 (23:03)	7 (17:41)
		4 6 3	3 5 3	3 4 4	3 3 5	3 2 6	3 1 7	3 9 8	3 8 9	3 7 1	3 6 2	3 5 3	3 4 4

	Jan	Feb	March	April	May	June	July	Aug	Sept	Oct	Nov	Dec
1971	6 (06:54)	4 (06:02)	6 (16:23)	4 (23:00)	5 (18:25)	6 (00:26)	7 (13:30)	8 (00:56)	8 (05:56)	8 (23:54)	8 (05:01)	7 (23:43)
	3 3 5	2 2 5	2 1 6	2 9 7	2 8 8	2 7 9	2 6 1	2 5 2	2 4 3	2 3 4	2 2 5	2 1 6
1972	6 (12:56)	5 (02:18)	5 (22:15)	4 (05:15)	5 (00:05)	5 (07:11)	6 (19:03)	7 (06:29)	7 (12:19)	8 (05:31)	7 (10:44)	7 (05:29)
	2 9 7	1 8 7	1 7 8	1 6 9	1 5 1	1 4 2	1 3 3	1 2 4	1 1 5	1 9 6	1 8 7	1 7 8
1973	5 (18:45)	4 (08:06)	6 (04:04)	4 (10:53)	5 (06:31)	5 (12:39)	7 (00:30)	7 (13:05)	7 (17:51)	8 (11:09)	7 (16:33)	7 (11:24)
	1 6 9	9 5 9	9 4 1	9 3 2	9 2 3	9 1 4	9 9 5	9 8 6	9 7 7	9 6 8	9 5 9	9 4 1
1974	6 (00:23)	4 (14:04)	6 (09:57)	4 (16:37)	5 (12:06)	5 (18:07)	7 (07:11)	7 (18:32)	7 (23:25)	8 (17:17)	7 (22:23)	7 (17:08)
	9 3 2	8 2 2	8 1 3	8 9 4	8 8 5	8 7 6	8 6 7	8 5 8	8 4 9	8 3 1	8 2 2	8 1 3
1975	6 (06:26)	4 (20:07)	6 (15:55)	4 (22:26)	5 (17:22)	5 (23:41)	7 (12:41)	8 (00:05)	8 (05:01)	8 (22:59)	8 (04:07)	7 (22:53)
	8 9 4	7 8 4	7 7 5	7 6 6	7 5 7	7 4 8	7 3 9	7 2 1	7 1 2	7 9 3	7 8 4	7 7 5
1976	6 (12:11)	5 (01:37)	5 (21:36)	4 (04:34)	4 (23:21)	5 (06:23)	6 (18:14)	7 (05:41)	7 (11:33)	8 (04:48)	7 (10:02)	7 (04:51)
	7 6 6	6 5 6	6 4 7	6 3 8	6 2 9	6 1 1	6 9 2	6 8 3	6 7 4	6 6 5	6 5 6	6 4 7
1977	5 (18:09)	4 (07:34)	6 (03:36)	4 (10:25)	5 (06:02)	5 (12:06)	6 (23:52)	7 (12:24)	7 (17:09)	8 (10:19)	7 (15:52)	7 (10:44)
	6 3 8	5 2 8	5 1 9	5 9 1	5 8 2	5 7 3	5 6 4	5 5 5	5 4 6	5 3 7	5 2 8	5 1 9
1978	5 (23:46)	4 (13:31)	6 (09:28)	4 (16:12)	5 (11:42)	5 (17:41)	7 (05:24)	7 (17:55)	7 (22:44)	8 (16:34)	7 (21:39)	7 (16:37)
	5 9 1	4 8 1	4 7 2	4 6 3	4 5 4	4 4 5	4 3 6	4 2 7	4 1 8	4 9 9	4 8 1	4 7 2
1979	6 (05:39)	4 (19:19)	6 (15:09)	4 (21:44)	5 (17:07)	5 (23:06)	7 (12:08)	7 (23:32)	8 (04:28)	8 (22:27)	8 (03:37)	7 (22:24)
	4 6 3	3 5 3	3 4 4	3 3 5	3 2 6	3 1 7	3 9 8	3 8 9	3 7 1	3 6 2	3 5 3	3 4 4
1980	6 (11:41)	5 (01:07)	5 (21:04)	4 (04:02)	4 (22:52)	5 (05:57)	6 (17:48)	7 (05:13)	7 (10:11)	8 (04:10)	7 (09:23)	7 (04:11)
	3 3 5	2 2 5	2 1 6	2 9 7	2 8 8	2 7 9	2 6 1	2 5 2	2 4 3	2 3 4	2 2 5	2 1 6
1981	5 (17:31)	4 (06:56)	6 (02:57)	4 (09:46)	5 (05:22)	5 (11:29)	6 (23:18)	7 (11:53)	7 (16:38)	8 (09:53)	7 (15:14)	7 (10:04)
	2 9 7	1 8 7	1 7 8	1 6 9	1 5 1	1 4 2	1 3 3	1 2 4	1 1 5	1 9 6	1 8 7	1 7 8
1982	5 (23:05)	4 (12:49)	6 (08:45)	4 (15:26)	5 (10:54)	5 (16:55)	7 (04:42)	7 (17:21)	7 (22:14)	8 (16:06)	7 (21:10)	7 (16:04)
	1 6 9	9 5 9	9 4 1	9 3 2	9 2 3	9 1 4	9 9 5	9 8 6	9 7 7	9 6 8	9 5 9	9 4 1
1983	6 (05:06)	4 (18:46)	6 (14:36)	4 (21:11)	5 (16:33)	5 (22:28)	7 (11:28)	7 (22:53)	8 (03:51)	8 (21:49)	8 (02:57)	7 (21:40)
	9 3 2	8 2 2	8 1 3	8 9 4	8 8 5	8 7 6	8 6 7	8 5 8	8 4 9	8 3 1	8 2 2	8 1 3
1984	6 (10:54)	5 (00:16)	6 (20:13)	4 (03:11)	5 (22:01)	5 (05:04)	6 (16:56)	7 (04:24)	7 (09:27)	8 (03:33)	7 (08:49)	7 (03:37)
	8 9 4	7 8 4	7 7 5	7 6 6	7 5 7	7 4 8	7 3 9	7 2 1	7 1 2	7 9 3	7 8 4	7 7 5
1985	5 (16:52)	4 (06:12)	6 (02:08)	4 (08:55)	5 (04:32)	5 (10:38)	6 (22:27)	7 (11:02)	7 (15:49)	8 (09:09)	7 (14:33)	7 (09:29)
	7 6 6	6 5 6	6 4 7	6 3 8	6 2 9	6 1 1	6 9 2	6 8 3	6 7 4	6 6 5	6 5 6	6 4 7
1986	5 (22:30)	4 (12:11)	6 (08:03)	4 (14:41)	5 (10:07)	5 (16:07)	7 (03:52)	7 (16:28)	7 (21:19)	8 (15:12)	7 (20:18)	7 (15:18)
	6 3 8	5 2 8	5 1 9	5 9 1	5 8 2	5 7 3	5 6 4	5 5 5	5 4 6	5 3 7	5 2 8	5 1 9
1987	6 (04:20)	4 (17:58)	6 (13:43)	4 (20:12)	5 (15:30)	5 (21:25)	7 (10:27)	7 (21:54)	8 (02:56)	8 (20:58)	8 (02:10)	7 (20:57)
	5 9 1	4 8 1	4 7 2	4 6 3	4 5 4	4 4 5	4 3 6	4 2 7	4 1 8	4 9 9	4 8 1	4 7 2

Find your own numbers from the magic square

Feng shui basics

	Jan	Feb	March	April	May	June	July	Aug	Sept	Oct	Nov	Dec
1988	6 (10:15) 4 6 3	4 (23:40) 3 5 3	5 (19:34) 3 4 4	4 (02:29) 3 3 5	4 (21:12) 3 2 6	5 (03:03) 3 1 7	6 (16:03) 3 9 8	7 (03:29) 3 8 9	7 (08:32) 3 7 1	8 (02:37) 3 6 2	7 (07:53) 3 5 3	7 (02:43) 3 4 4
1989	5 (16:03) 3 3 5	4 (05:27) 2 2 5	6 (01:26) 2 1 6	4 (08:13) 2 9 7	5 (03:45) 2 8 8	5 (09:47) 2 7 9	6 (21:32) 2 6 1	7 (10:04) 2 5 2	7 (14:52) 2 4 3	8 (08:13) 2 3 4	7 (13:37) 2 2 5	7 (08:33) 2 1 6
1990	5 (21:34) 2 9 7	4 (11:17) 1 8 7	6 (07:10) 1 7 8	4 (13:48) 1 6 9	5 (09:14) 1 5 1	5 (15:11) 1 4 2	7 (02:55) 1 3 3	7 (15:30) 1 2 4	7 (20:24) 1 1 5	8 (14:20) 1 9 6	7 (19:29) 1 8 7	7 (14:29) 1 7 8
1991	6 (03:34) 1 6 9	7 (17:14) 9 5 9	6 (13:02) 9 4 1	4 (19:33) 9 3 2	5 (14:53) 9 2 3	5 (20:46) 9 1 4	7 (09:44) 9 9 5	7 (21:06) 9 8 6	8 (02:02) 9 7 7	8 (20:01) 9 6 8	8 (01:13) 9 5 9	7 (20:01) 9 4 1
1992	6 (09:20) 9 3 2	4 (22:45) 8 2 2	5 (18:41) 8 1 3	4 (01:36) 8 9 4	4 (20:22) 8 8 5	5 (02:14) 8 7 6	6 (15:13) 8 6 7	7 (02:39) 8 5 8	7 (07:40) 8 4 9	8 (01:44) 8 3 1	7 (07:01) 8 2 2	7 (01:52) 8 1 3
1993	5 (15:12) 8 9 4	4 (04:37) 7 8 4	6 (00:35) 7 7 5	4 (07:21) 7 6 6	5 (02:55) 7 5 7	5 (08:59) 7 4 8	6 (20:46) 7 3 9	7 (09:21) 7 2 1	7 (14:08) 7 1 2	8 (07:27) 7 9 3	7 (12:49) 7 8 4	7 (07:45) 7 7 5
1994	5 (20:49) 7 6 6	4 (10:33) 6 5 6	6 (06:29) 6 4 7	4 (13:08) 6 3 8	5 (08:34) 6 2 9	5 (14:32) 6 1 1	7 (02:16) 6 9 2	7 (14:51) 6 8 3	7 (19:43) 6 7 4	8 (13:36) 6 6 5	7 (18:41) 6 5 6	7 (13:38) 6 4 7
1995	6 (02:39) 6 3 8	4 (16:19) 5 2 8	6 (12:06) 5 1 9	4 (18:38) 5 9 1	5 (13:58) 5 8 2	5 (19:53) 5 7 3	7 (08:54) 5 6 4	7 (20:22) 5 5 5	8 (01:24) 5 4 6	8 (19:27) 5 3 7	8 (00:40) 5 2 8	7 (19:27) 5 1 9
1996	6 (08:42) 5 9 1	4 (22:04) 4 8 1	5 (17:58) 4 7 2	4 (00:54) 4 6 3	4 (19:40) 4 5 4	5 (01:34) 4 4 5	6 (14:35) 4 3 6	7 (02:02) 4 2 7	7 (07:06) 4 1 8	8 (01:12) 4 9 9	7 (06:31) 4 8 1	7 (01:22) 4 7 2
1997	5 (14:40) 4 6 3	4 (04:01) 3 5 3	5 (23:57) 3 4 4	4 (06:41) 3 3 5	5 (01:22) 3 2 6	5 (08:18) 3 1 7	6 (20:07) 3 9 8	7 (07:34) 3 8 9	7 (13:30) 3 7 1	8 (06:52) 3 6 2	7 (12:18) 3 5 3	7 (07:16) 3 4 4
1998	5 (20:18) 3 3 5	4 (09:59) 2 2 5	6 (05:48) 2 1 6	4 (12:22) 2 9 7	5 (07:45) 2 8 8	5 (13:43) 2 7 9	7 (01:29) 2 6 1	7 (14:08) 2 5 2	7 (19:05) 2 4 3	8 (12:36) 2 3 4	7 (18:14) 2 2 5	7 (13:16) 2 1 6
1999	6 (02:22) 2 9 7	4 (16:02) 1 8 7	6 (11:47) 1 7 8	4 (18:14) 1 6 9	5 (13:30) 1 5 1	5 (19:21) 1 4 2	7 (08:21) 1 3 3	7 (19:46) 1 2 4	8 (00:47) 1 1 5	8 (18:49) 1 9 6	8 (00:03) 1 8 7	7 (18:52) 1 7 8
2000	6 (08:12) 1 6 9	4 (21:36) 9 5 9	5 (17:32) 9 4 1	3 (23:57) 9 3 2	4 (19:08) 9 2 3	5 (00:56) 9 1 4	6 (13:51) 9 9 5	7 (01:19) 9 8 6	7 (06:23) 9 7 7	8 (00:33) 9 6 8	7 (05:52) 9 5 9	7 (00:45) 9 4 1
2001	5 (14:05) 9 3 2	4 (03:29) 8 2 2	5 (23:26) 8 1 3	4 (06:10) 8 9 4	5 (00:48) 8 8 5	5 (07:42) 8 7 6	6 (19:26) 8 6 7	7 (06:52) 8 5 8	7 (12:50) 8 4 9	8 (06:14) 8 3 1	7 (11:41) 8 2 2	7 (06:41) 8 1 3
2002	5 (19:45) 8 9 4	4 (09:27) 7 8 4	6 (05:20) 7 7 5	4 (11:57) 7 6 6	5 (07:21) 7 5 7	5 (13:17) 7 4 8	7 (00:59) 7 3 9	7 (13:31) 7 2 1	7 (18:23) 7 1 2	8 (11:52) 7 9 3	7 (17:29) 7 8 4	7 (12:30) 7 7 5
2003	6 (01:34) 7 6 6	4 (15:12) 6 5 6	6 (10:56) 6 4 7	4 (17:25) 6 3 8	5 (12:42) 6 2 9	5 (18:35) 6 1 1	7 (07:35) 6 9 2	7 (18:59) 6 8 3	8 (00:00) 6 7 4	8 (18:03) 6 6 5	7 (23:19) 6 5 6	7 (18:10) 6 4 7
2004	6 (07:29) 6 3 8	3 (21:09) 5 2 8	5 (16:45) 5 1 9	3 (23:08) 5 9 1	4 (18:21) 5 8 2	5 (00:12) 5 7 3	6 (13:12) 5 6 4	7 (00:38) 5 5 5	7 (05:40) 5 4 6	7 (23:46) 5 3 7	7 (05:04) 5 2 8	6 (23:57) 5 1 9

	Jan	Feb	March	April	May	June	July	Aug	Sept	Oct	Nov	Dec
2005	5 (13:18) 5 9 1	4 (02:43) 4 8 1	5 (22:34) 4 7 2	4 (05:22) 4 6 3	4 (23:59) 4 5 4	5 (06:53) 4 4 5	6 (18:39) 4 3 6	7 (06:06) 4 2 7	7 (12:02) 4 1 8	8 (05:23) 4 9 9	7 (10:47) 4 8 1	7 (05:44) 4 7 2
2006	5 (18:51) 4 6 3	4 (08:30) 3 5 3	6 (04:21) 3 4 4	4 (10:56) 3 3 5	5 (06:17) 3 2 6	5 (12:12) 3 1 7	6 (23:56) 3 9 8	7 (12:35) 3 8 9	7 (17:32) 3 7 1	8 (11:04) 3 6 2	7 (16:42) 3 5 3	7 (11:41) 3 4 4
2007	6 (00:45) 3 3 5	4 (14:23) 2 2 5	6 (10:09) 2 1 6	4 (16:38) 2 9 7	5 (11:54) 2 8 8	5 (17:45) 2 7 9	7 (05:29) 2 6 1	7 (18:09) 2 5 2	7 (23:11) 2 4 3	8 (17:15) 2 3 4	7 (22:30) 2 2 5	7 (17:19) 2 1 6
2008	6 (06:35) 2 9 7	4 (20:10) 1 8 7	5 (15:49) 1 7 8	3 (22:13) 1 6 9	4 (17:25) 1 5 1	4 (23:14) 1 4 2	6 (12:11) 1 3 3	6 (23:38) 1 2 4	7 (04:43) 1 1 5	7 (22:54) 1 9 6	7 (04:16) 1 8 7	6 (23:10) 1 7 8
2009	5 (12:29) 1 6 9	4 (01:49) 9 5 9	5 (21:36) 9 4 1	4 (04:22) 9 3 2	4 (22:59) 9 2 3	5 (05:53) 9 1 4	6 (17:39) 9 9 5	7 (05:06) 9 8 6	7 (10:14) 9 7 7	8 (04:30) 9 6 8	7 (10:01) 9 5 9	7 (05:03) 9 4 1
2010	5 (18:28) 9 3 2	4 (07:50) 8 2 2	6 (03:39) 8 1 3	4 (10:12) 8 9 4	5 (05:32) 8 8 5	5 (11:26) 8 7 6	6 (23:10) 8 6 7	7 (11:46) 8 5 8	7 (16:40) 8 4 9	8 (10:11) 8 3 1	7 (15:49) 8 2 2	7 (10:53) 8 1 3
2011	5 (23:59) 8 9 4	4 (13:39) 7 8 4	6 (09:21) 7 7 5	4 (15:47) 7 6 6	5 (10:59) 7 5 7	5 (16:49) 7 4 8	7 (04:32) 7 3 9	7 (17:14) 7 2 1	7 (22:18) 7 1 2	8 (16:24) 7 9 3	7 (21:41) 7 8 4	7 (16:46) 7 7 5
2012	6 (05:53) 7 6 6	4 (19:30) 6 5 6	5 (15:11) 6 4 7	3 (21:33) 6 3 8	4 (16:42) 6 2 9	4 (22:29) 6 1 1	6 (11:27) 6 9 2	6 (22:54) 6 8 3	7 (03:59) 6 7 4	7 (22:10) 6 6 5	7 (03:31) 6 5 6	6 (22:26) 6 4 7
2013	5 (11:48) 6 3 8	4 (01:12) 5 2 8	5 (21:04) 5 1 9	4 (03:52) 5 9 1	4 (22:28) 5 8 2	5 (05:19) 5 7 3	6 (17:03) 5 6 4	7 (04:28) 5 5 5	7 (09:35) 5 4 6	8 (03:50) 5 3 7	7 (09:19) 5 2 8	7 (04:19) 5 1 9
2014	5 (17:43) 5 9 1	4 (07:05) 4 8 1	6 (02:55) 4 7 2	4 (09:29) 4 6 3	5 (04:49) 4 5 4	5 (10:43) 4 4 5	6 (22:25) 4 3 6	7 (11:01) 4 2 7	7 (15:58) 4 1 8	8 (09:32) 4 9 9	7 (15:14) 4 8 1	7 (10:18) 4 7 2
2015	5 (23:24) 4 6 3	4 (13:03) 3 5 3	6 (08:47) 3 4 4	4 (15:14) 3 3 5	5 (10:29) 3 2 6	5 (16:20) 3 1 7	7 (04:04) 3 9 8	7 (16:43) 3 8 9	7 (21:44) 3 7 1	8 (15:48) 3 6 2	7 (21:05) 3 5 3	7 (16:11) 3 4 4
2016	6 (05:17) 3 3 5	4 (18:55) 2 2 5	5 (14:34) 2 1 6	3 (20:56) 2 9 7	4 (16:06) 2 8 8	4 (21:55) 2 7 9	6 (10:52) 2 6 1	6 (22:19) 2 5 2	7 (03:23) 2 4 3	7 (21:32) 2 3 4	7 (02:53) 2 2 5	6 (21:48) 2 1 6
2017	5 (11:09) 2 9 7	4 (00:33) 1 8 7	5 (20:22) 1 7 8	4 (03:07) 1 6 9	4 (21:42) 1 5 1	5 (03:25) 1 4 2	6 (16:21) 1 3 3	7 (03:48) 1 2 4	7 (08:58) 1 1 5	8 (03:14) 1 9 6	7 (08:42) 1 8 7	7 (03:43) 1 7 8

WHAT YOUR NUMBERS MEAN

Nine ki year number (**5** 5 5)

Your year number relates to your basic character and deepest chi. This provides information on how you will progress in life. For example, someone with the year number 1 may find their life builds up slowly, similar to the way a small brook grows into a river. The year number helps define the best long-term career for you, your basic values in life and your deepest nature.

YEAR NUMBER	PROGRESS	CAREER QUALITIES	DEEPEST NATURE
1	Build up over long term, flexible	Original, objective	Independent, sexual
2	Steady, consistent	Caring, improve quality	Practical, home maker
3	Quick start, make things happen	Accurate, analytical	Ambitious, enthusiastic
4	Harmonious, forward	Spread ideas, inventive	Determined, persistent
5	Changeable, attract opportunities	Prime mover, attract attention	Sense of justice, changeable
6	Long-term plans, keep going	Organization, leadership	Showing integrity, responsible
7	Seek comfort, motivated by wealth	Stylish, financially aware	Content, playful
8	Seek new opportunities, sudden changes	Speculation, motivated	Hard-working, insightful
9	Emotionally led, networking	Public recognition, self-expression	Passionate, social

Nine ki month number (5 **5** 5)

This number has the greatest influence on your relationships, as it relates to the way you communicate, express your ideas and feel emotionally.

A combination that works well emotionally will lead to a deeper, more satisfying relationship. When a relationship does not thrive, you may feel that neither person understands the other, leading to a situation where every little upset creates a deeper rift. The emotions associated with your nine ki month number affect you more deeply and more frequently than other emotions. Look up your strongest emotional traits in the chart below. Compare them with those of your lover.

MONTH NUMBER	THINKING	COMMUNICATION	EMOTIONS
1	Objective, independent	Fluid, open	Deep, affectionate
2	Methodical, practical	Considerate, tactful	Caring, settled
3	Focused, precise	Frank, reasoned	Confident, assertive
4	Imaginative, innovative	Persuasive, persistent	Gentle, sensitive
5	Black and white, well thought-out	Powerful, understated	Changeable, determined
6	Organized, intuitive	Honest, cautious	Self-controlled, mature
7	Focused on end result, positive	Charming, stylish	Playful, joyous
8	Competitive, quick	Clear, direct	Outgoing, motivated
9	Fast, emotionally led	Passionate, expressive	Fiery, impulsive

Nine ki axis number (5 5 **5**)

This number relates to your most superficial chi, and is often people's first impression of you. It also illustrates how you do things. For this reason it provides useful information about the way you work. Many people may know you according to your superficial chi, since this is the energy that first stands out when someone meets you. Usually they soon begin to relate to you in terms of your month energy. But it is only when they get to know you better that they can really understand you in terms of your deeper year number. If the axis number is different from the deeper energies, you can switch into being a very different person at work compared to the person you are at home.

AXIS NUMBER	FIRST IMPRESSION	WORK QUALITIES
1	Laid-back, easy-going	Objective, independent
2	Considerate, friendly	Thorough, team worker
3	Solution-orientated, knowledgeable	Accurate, enthusiastic
4	Gentle, full of interesting ideas	Creative, possessing a wealth of ideas
5	Able to put up a strong front, confrontational	Having strong ideas, desiring to be in charge
6	Serious, formal	Well-organized, in control
7	Charming, stylish	Focused on end result, financially motivated
8	Direct, inquisitive	Motivated by goals, getting on with the job
9	Socially aware, intelligent	Seeking useful connections, aware of reputation

THE TIMING OF EVENTS

Each year the pattern of the magic square changes. To find the appropriate chart for any particular year, look at the table on page 44. Find the year in which you are interested, and then look for the year number from February onwards. For example, the year number for 2006 is 3. So find the magic square on page 43 with the year number in which you are interested in the centre. Now locate your own year number and see where it lies in the year chart. Someone with the year number 1, for instance, will be in the east in 2006. The chi of that position on the chart will influence you for that year, making it easier for you to achieve certain things in life.

You can apply the same principle to each month. Look for the month in which you are interested on page 44–9 and make a note of the middle, month number. Remember that the months do not start at the same time as ours, so for the first few days you may need to use the previous month. Find the chart on page 43 with the same month number in the centre and look for the position of your year number.

Important events

The chi you take in during any important event will stay with you, potentially for many years. For example, getting married can bring about a long-lasting shift in your chi. Conversely, if you start a relationship when one or both of you are going through a difficult time, you may set up more destructive patterns of behaviour towards each other, which then becomes a recurring theme as the relationship progresses.

Similarly, if you begin a new business at a favourable time and enjoy success initially, you should find it is easy to ride through any later difficulties, based on the momentum of your earlier successes.

Opposite 5

You need to be careful when your year number is opposite the powerful force of 5. For example, in the year 2006, 5 is to the west. This would mean that 1, situated in the east, is opposite 5. In such cases it is easy to feel blocked, so it would be wiser to position yourself so that opportunities come to you, rather than pushing too hard for anything.

Business cycle

The nine phases described above can be put into a business cycle, which reflects the different chronological phases that you would go through.

- **North** New original ideas
- **South-west** Research and development
- **East** Putting the ideas into action
- **South-east** Expansion and marketing
- **Centre** Attracting attention
- **North-west** Organization and planning ahead
- **West** Increasing profitability and raising finance
- **North-east** Being competitive and direct
- **South** Promotion and sales

If you can catch and harmonize with one of these nine ki cycles you will experience that feeling of being on a roll where things fall into place with very little effort.

Nine ki phases and emotions

Look at the list below to see what effect each of the nine phases could have on you emotionally. You can apply these to a year or to a month.

DIRECTION	HELPS	RISKS
East	Confidence	Anger
	Self-esteem	Irritability
	Ambition	Impatience
	Enthusiasm	Making mistakes
South-east	Persistence	Not letting go
	Inspiration	Hypersensitivity
	Imagination	Daydreaming
	Getting new ideas	Unrealistic ideas
South	Passion	Argumentativeness
	Self-expression	Stress
	Generosity	Hysteria
	Pride	Separation
South-west	Realism	Caution
	Practicality	Feeling stuck
	Deeper relationships	Dependency
	Improving quality	Jealousy

Nine phases of a relationship

• **East** Greater enthusiasm to do things; but there is a risk of feeling irritable, short-tempered and less inclined to listen.

• **South-east** Creates a more harmonious relationship, avoiding confrontation; it is easier to feel positive about your relationship.

• **Centre** Attracts more attention; but there is a risk of being unsure of your feelings towards your lover.

• **North-west** Greater confidence to move on to a more serious and permanent footing; but you can be judgemental and self-righteous.

• **West** More romantic and fun; physical pleasure will be more important, but you may not take your lover seriously.

• **North-east** You can do a lot together, but you may get rid of things that no longer work for you; you are better able to stand your ground.

• **South** Passionate, warm and generous; but you can feel argumentative, reacting strongly if your pride is hurt, leading to a separation.

• **North** Ideal for sex, affection and exploring each other's deeper side; but you can be more aloof and need your own space.

• **South-west** Easier to feel close, improve the quality or your relationship and make things work in the long term; but you could lose the excitement and spontaneity.

Use the table opposite for a quick reference to the qualities of each phase. Find the direction of your year number within the relevant chart and then locate that direction in the table.

DIRECTION	HELPS	RISKS
West	Romance	Depression
	Contentment	Lack of motivation
	Playfulness	Irresponsibility
	Enjoyment of pleasures	Immaturity
North-west	Self-control	Arrogance
	Self-assuredness	Self-righteousness
	Intuition	Being judgemental
	Wisdom	Condescension
North	Sexual vitality	Worry
	Spirituality	Insecurity
	Finding inner peace	Isolation
	Independence	Loneliness
North-east	Motivation	Greed
	Feeling competitive	Feeling obsessive
	Fighting spirit	Feeling on edge
	Feeling clear-minded	Being critical
Centre	Attract opportunities	Changing mind
	Being centre of attention	Confrontation
	Developing opinions	Making rash decisions
	Feeling empowered	Self-obsession

YOUR BEST DIRECTIONS

Each year and month, certain directions will be more favourable to your year chi. Imagine that you want to sail across the sea: you would first need to study the tides and the direction of the prevailing winds so that you could choose the ideal time to begin your journey. Similarly, you can find when the best feng shui (wind and water) conditions arise to make your move. This primarily applies to a house move, but can also have a significant influence on setting up a new business or finding a new job. The same principle applies to making changes to your home.

How to find your best directions

To find your best directions, look at the chart on page 44–49 to make a note of your year number, and the year and month numbers of the time when you want to move. Then go to page 43 and make a copy of the charts with the same year and month numbers in the centre as when you want to move.

1 Cross off the axis (the straight line of three numbers going through the centre of the square, whether vertically, horizontally or diagonally) with the number 5 in it. Ignore this step if the month or year has 5 in the centre. Moving towards the number 5 can be unpredictable – small problems may run out of control. Moving away from it can weaken your chi, resulting in greater vulnerability to accidents and injuries.

2 Cross off the axis with your own year number. Moving towards your year number is like trying to push two magnets together when both poles have the same charge – risking confusion and the feeling that life is becoming unnecessarily complicated. Moving away from your year number is almost like leaving a part of yourself behind, with the result that you can miss your old home and feel empty.

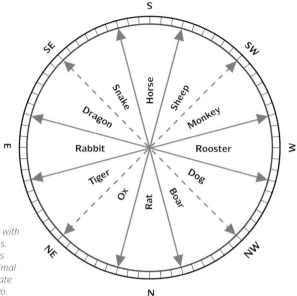

The 12 Chinese animals are fused with the eight directions. The cardinal points each have one animal and the intermediate directions have two.

3 Cross off the direction that is opposite the active animal for that year or month (see the chart). Moving away from the active animal can produce a deficiency of chi, with the result that things seem almost to happen, but run out of steam at the last moment.

4 Cross off the direction that has the number that is opposite its normal position, when 5 is in the centre (for example, when 9 is in the centre of the magic square,

7 is in the east – opposite its normal position of west). Ignore this step if the year or month chart has 5 in the centre. When moving towards a number that is opposite its normal position on the chart, you may find that events are less likely to go as planned.

5 Look at the remaining directions to see those that are generally favourable to you.

BASIC RULES

- *The influence of the year will be greater than that of the month.*

- *The direction in which you move is from the place you have been sleeping in for at least three months to the next destination in which you will sleep for three months. It is not the route that you choose in order to get there.*

- *To establish yourself in the new chi, you need to sleep every night in the new location for at least two months.*

- *The greater the distance you move, the stronger and quicker the influence.*

- *When working out directions for families, concentrate on the year numbers of the parents.*

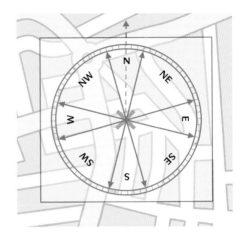

Applying the eight directions to a map

Take a map and mark your home with an X. Draw a line from your home towards north (usually at the top of the page). Place your transparency of the eight directions (see pages 112–115) so that the centre is over your home and so that north on the transparency is aligned with the line you have just drawn. This will show you the eight directions from your home. The same can be done with a world map for long-distance travel.

When to make changes to your home

The principles are the same as finding the best time to move house. This applies to building an extension, adding a conservatory, making renovations and implementing feng shui cures. For major work, it is best to wait for a suitable year, but for most other alterations to your home it is sufficient to find a favourable month.

1 Place the transparency of the eight directions (see pages 112–115) over your floor plan (see pages 108–111) to see in which direction the change is going to take place.

2 Write out the chart for the current month and cross off the directions that are not suitable.

3 If the direction of the changes has not been crossed off, begin the changes before the month ends. If the direction has been crossed off, repeat the process for the next month and carry on until you find a month when that direction is positive.

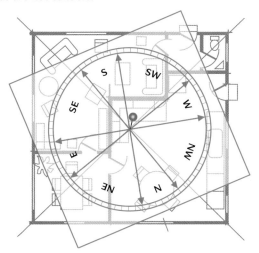

Feng shui basics

PUT IT ALL TOGETHER

One way to apply everything you have learnt so far is to find the best place to sit in your home.

Look at the room you want to sit in, to sense where the chi would be calmest. You would not want to sit close to a door, a sharp protruding corner or a large window. Think in terms of yin and yang – look for soft, calm (yin) areas to relax in, or bright, colourful (yang) areas to feel stimulated in.

Try to sense the chi that is present. Strong vertical forms, high ceilings and wooden surfaces generate more 'upward' wood chi. Sunny exposure, bright reds or purples and a fireplace all radiate more fiery chi. Low soft spaces, with earthy colours and horizontal forms, contain more soil chi. Hard surfaces, metal objects and grey or silver colours combine to create inward metal chi. Flowing shapes, glass and translucent finishes produce a quieter, water-chi atmosphere.

Consider options that will allow you to sit with your back to a wall (protected by the tortoise) and your front open to as much of the room as possible (so that the chi of the phoenix can rise up in front of you). Low objects on either side will provide the supporting chi of the dragon and tiger.

Finally, take a compass to establish which direction you will be facing in your different sitting options. The direction that you face will help you absorb more of that particular chi – so facing east, for instance, will help you absorb more eastern chi.

Directional qualities

Sitting with your back to a wall facing a direction with helpful chi will put you in a strong position.

• **East** This is positive and confident chi, but not particularly relaxing; it can boost your self-esteem a little.

• **South-east** Great for daydreaming and letting your imagination run wild; also helpful for thinking about the future.

• **South** Excellent for feeling expressive, sociable, mentally stimulated and outgoing, but not particularly relaxing.

• **South-west** This chi gets your feet securely back on the ground, but it can bring your energy levels down, if your head is too busy.

• **West** Good for feeling content, romantic and at ease with yourself, but avoid this direction when you feel withdrawn or low.

• **North-west** Helpful for reviewing your life and drawing on your wisdom or intuition, but avoid it if you are a control freak.

• **North** Ideal for rest and relaxation – it helps you calm down and go with the flow; also good for meditation.

• **North-east** Helpful for greater mental clarity or for being decisive, but it can be too sharp and piercing to be relaxing.

THE BUILDING BLOCKS OF FENG SHUI

USE DESIGN ELEMENTS TO CHANGE THE ATMOSPHERE OF A SPACE

Whenever you want to redecorate, renovate or design your own home, you have an amazing opportunity to create an atmosphere that really works for you. This is when you can go mad choosing flooring, painting walls and selecting lighting and furniture. In this mode, feng shui is all about making more informed choices, so every decision is taken knowing the effect that it will have on the people living there. The focus is solely on the occupants, rather than on the style of the home.

In one sense, this is really preventative feng shui, because rather than trying to solve a problem using feng shui, you have a chance to avoid doing something that will have an adverse influence on your life. If your life is going well, you do not want to do anything to upset it.

If you are fortunate enough to be able to design your own home, you can even specify the layout of the rooms, their

A glass table and a polished floor will speed up the flow of chi making this a more yang, dynamic space to sit.

proportions and the materials with which your new house will be built. You may even be able to decide which direction it faces, and therefore the kind of chi that will pour into the front of your home.

Soft yin fabrics mixed with bright yang colours make this space visually stimulating.

DESIGN TIPS

- *Special features* Think through how you will bring in many special feng shui features, such as plants, a water feature or candles. In this way everything has its own special place in your home.

- *Be flexible* Whether your project is small or large, it is always best to make each room as flexible as possible and to keep built-in furniture to a minimum. For example, it is always good to have two or three options in terms of where you can place your bed, but built-in wardrobes can soon limit this to one. If this position turns out not to be beneficial to you, subsequent changes can be expensive. Try to design rooms using free-standing furniture and allow yourself the freedom to move things around at a later date.

- *Consider the materials you will be using* Many modern materials can give off toxic fumes for years after you have installed them. Try using organic paints; solid wood for flooring, surfaces and furniture; and pure wool or cotton for fabrics; and minimize the use of plastics.

COLOURS

The colours that you use to decorate your home will have a significant influence on its chi, because each colour reflects different light frequencies back into the room, filling it with either faster or slower chi. As these light frequencies travel through your outer chi field, they also change the way your own chi moves, resulting in different feelings and thoughts.

CUSHIONS

Use cushions to bring colour into a room – and play around with them, placing them in different parts of the room until you find the arrangement you like best.

Yin and yang colours

Bright reds, yellows and oranges help you feel more active, stimulated and yang. Pale colours, such as light blues and greens, help you feel more peaceful, calm and yin.

Large plain blocks of bright colour are most yang, although you can also make a room feel more yang using straight-line patterns, such as checks or a grid. Wavy lines or irregular forms break up the flow of chi, making it more yin.

This room is decorated with stimulating yang colours.

This charts shows all the colours that are harmonious to a direction. Use it as a guide for decorating or adding colour to your home.

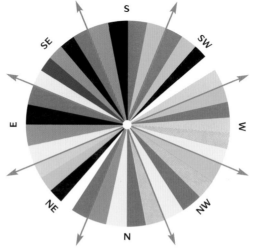

Eight directions

Look at the descriptions of the eight directions, starting on page 36. Find a direction that has the properties you need more of, and then see which colour is associated with it. For example, to feel more expressive and sociable, you need more southern chi. The colour that helps activate this energy is bright purple.

Use the appropriate colour in the part of your home that it relates to. For instance, use bright purple in the south part of your home. Use the transparency of the eight directions (see pages 112–115) to establish which colours to use in different rooms. Try to include the colour of each direction in its most powerful place, although you can also use other colours with it. So you might have a white room in the south, with just a few bright purple touches.

When you are ready to paint, put large test patches on the wall and live with them for a few days to see how you feel. The stronger the colour, the less you will need to change the energy of a room.

MATERIALS

The surfaces that you use in your home also define how the chi flows there. Careful selection of materials means that you can fine-tune the atmosphere of your house or apartment. Big surface areas, such as flooring, will have the greatest influence, and it is worth taking great care over the materials you use.

Natural materials tend to carry chi more easily than synthetic materials, and help it circulate well throughout your home. An example of this is wood, where the chi continues to flow along the grain. Many synthetic materials block the passage of chi, risking the creation of stagnant spaces within your home. In addition, some synthetic materials, such as nylon carpets, build up a charge of static electricity that interferes with your superficial chi.

The soft fabric of the sofa slows the chi whilst the wood floor speeds it up, creating a more balanced chi flow.

Yin and yang materials

Rough-textured surfaces (such as a wool carpet) slow chi down, making it more yin, whereas hard, shiny, flat surfaces (such as glazed tiles) speed up the flow of chi, creating a more yang atmosphere.

WOOD MATERIALS

- Wicker

- Bamboo

- Seagrass

- Cork

- Wood

FIRE MATERIALS

- Glazed tile

- Fired stone

SOIL MATERIALS

- Carpet

- Fabric

- Rough soft stone

METAL MATERIALS

- Hard stone

- Metal

WATER MATERIALS

- Glass

- Mirror

The five elements

You can also think of materials in terms of the five elements (see page 30). Each type of material encourages a certain flow of chi. By applying the transparency of the eight directions (see pages 112–115), you can establish which materials naturally suit each part of your home. Using those materials will lead to a more harmonious exchange of chi and will develop distinct atmospheres in each part of your home.

This wardrobe adds more wood chi, the lamp fire chi and the low sofa soil chi to this corner.

LIGHTING

Lighting is a very flexible and immediate decorating tool. At the flick of a switch, you can change from a bright, yang environment to a soft, yin mood. Lights generally produce more fire chi, although different forms of lighting are associated with each of the five elements. You can often use free-standing lights to create the effect you want, thereby reducing the cost and keeping everything adaptable.

Yin and yang lighting

Any kind of diffused or reflected, indirect lighting tends to be more yin. For example, a light that reflects its beam off a wall or the ceiling is more yin than any kind of direct lighting. Lights that have a shade are more yin than those that expose a naked beam directly to a room. But a bright spotlight or halogen downlighter is more yang.

The five elements

Lighting may also be seen in terms of the five elements (see page 30).

• **Wood** If you want to create a more inspiring atmosphere, try using uplighters. This will also help your room feel taller and

Shaded lamps give off more diffused yin chi, helping to make a room feel more soft and cosy with a soil chi atmosphere.

High intensity spotlights produce yang chi and here, more concentrated metal chi in terms of the five elements.

roomier. A bright ceiling and slightly darker floor mirrors the relationship between sky and ground, making the interior lighting seem more natural. This is particularly good for rooms with low ceilings or oppressive beams.

• **Fire** Anything that creates an explosion of light, such as a large chandelier, is the ultimate expression of fire chi.

• **Soil** Soft table or floor lamps bring the energy down and generate a relaxing, intimate mood in the room. You can also use coloured lighting when you want to soften the atmosphere further.

• **Metal** To produce a more intense, concentrated appearance, use spotlights to pick out features in your room, such as flower arrangements, paintings and plants.

• **Water** A light source that constantly changes generates more water chi. This could be a coloured light projected onto a wall or a light shining through a shimmering cloth.

ADAPTABILITY

Remember to keep your lighting flexible and easy to control, so that you can quickly switch from one lighting theme to another.

SHAPES

The shapes or forms in a room further define how the chi behaves there. Long, straight lines allow the chi to flow faster, while sharp edges encourage swirling chi, and corners slow down stagnant chi. The shapes of the furniture alter the chi flow to a lesser extent. For example, rounded or curved objects allow chi to move more harmoniously and make it easier for you to feel relaxed.

Yin and yang shapes

Yang shapes are those that encourage chi to move faster and are therefore made up of straight lines and hard edges. A rectangular room with rectangular furniture stimulates clarity of thought and should help you feel more decisive.

Yin forms are curved, rounded and irregular, so an irregular-shaped room with a variety of rounded and curved furniture encourages chi to meander more slowly, making it easier to feel settled there. This type of room is generally better when you need to use your creativity and imagination.

Strong linear lines and shapes create a yang atmosphere where the feel is clean, orderly and functional.

The five elements

You can help to move chi in different directions using the shapes associated with the five elements.

• **Wood** Vertical lines, tall shapes and high ceilings encourage chi to move upwards, helping you to feel like taking on more and lifting the limits on what you can achieve.

• **Fire** Star shapes, zigzag lines and pyramid forms produce more fire chi. For instance, a pointed ceiling is mentally stimulating and makes it easier to express yourself.

• **Soil** Horizontal lines, squat flat forms and low ceilings create more soil chi. This makes it easier to connect with other people and focus on what is going on around you.

• **Metal** Arches, circles and domes bring more metal chi into a space. You will find that you can contain your chi better and can focus on completing things in your life.

• **Water** Wavy lines, irregular forms and abstract shapes generate water chi. Use these to help you feel more flexible and to dig deep for that original thought.

The half arch, stepped floor, irregular shape and mix of furniture give this room a water chi atmosphere.

THE FENG SHUI HOUSE

When designing a new home, you have the opportunity to lay out all the rooms in positions where the ambient chi suits the purpose of the room. In the example given here, the kitchen is situated in the south-east, where the wood chi is harmonious with both the fire of the cooker and the water of the sink. Similarly, the water in the bathroom is in harmony with the wood chi of the east.

The living and dining room is to the south and south-west, encouraging a social, interactive atmosphere. The south is ideal for entertaining and the south-west for settling down. The main entrance is to the west, bringing in more of the chi that helps you feel content, playful and romantic. The open central hallway gives the powerful chi of 5 (centre of the standard magic square) plenty of space to move.

The library/study is placed in the north-west, making it easier to be organized, feel in control and plan ahead. Putting the bedroom in the north makes it easier to benefit from this quiet chi for deep sleep. The dressing room in the north-east is in the location suited to feeling clear-minded and decisive. Alternatively, this would make a good location for playing games.

The boxes give ideas for the perfect colours, materials and shapes for each room. Each room mixes in other elements that are harmonious, using the five-element principles. For example, the fire of the south also includes wood and soil elements (written in italics).

WEST

Red, pink, *yellow, brown, beige, matt black, white, grey, cream.*

Metal, stone, *carpets, rugs, glass*

Circular, arched, *horizontal, wavy*

SOUTH-WEST

Black, *purple,* **yellow, brown,** *pink,* **grey**

Clay, fabrics, carpet, *tiles, metal, glazed earthenware.*

Horizontal, low, flat, *star, pointed, circular, arched.*

NORTH

Cream, clear varnish, *pale green, pale blue, pink, grey, Silver.*

Glass, *metal, stone, wood.*

Wavy, curved, irregular, *round, tall*

NORTH-WEST

Grey, silver, *black, yellow, red, cream.*

Metal, stone, *carpets, rugs, glass*

Circular, arched, *horizontal, wavy*

NORTH-EAST

White, *purple, yellow, black, pink, grey.*

Fabric, rugs, carpet, soft stone, *tiles, metal, glazed earthenware*

Horizontal, low, flat, *star, pointed, circular, arched.*

N

EAST

Bright green, *cream, dark green, blue, purple.*

Wood, *glass, glazed earthenware*

Tall, vertical, *wavy, pointed.*

SOUTH-EAST

Dark green, blue, *cream, bright green, purple.*

Wood, *glass, glazed earthenware*

Tall, vertical, *wavy, pointed.*

SOUTH

Purple, *green, blue,* **matt black,** *yellow, brown, beige.*

Wood, *glass, glazed earthenware*

Pointed, star, pyramid, *tall, horizontal*

Library

Bedroom

Dressing room

Entrance

Hallway

Bath-room

Living/dining room

Kitchen

USE REMEDIES TO SOLVE PERSONAL PROBLEMS

Curative feng shui is when you have identified a problem in your life and wish to use feng shui to help you solve it. In this scenario most people want as little disruption to their home – and to spend as little on remedies – as possible. The art of this style of feng shui is to be as accurate and specific as you can. It is a case of less is more.

Feng shui does not work like a magic pill, and by itself it will not make you wealthy, get you the perfect relationship or improve your health. You need to work at it and try to create the situations where any of these things can happen.

TIP

Remember that you cannot change another person – only yourself. So blaming another person will not lead to a situation that you can do anything about.

Writing your thoughts can be therapeutic in itself.

Get what you need out of feng shui

1 Imagine that you are at the end of your life. You are feeling content and satisfied as you prepare to move on from this material world. You have completed everything. Try to visualize, to feel and to hear what it would be like to have reached this state.

2 Think about what you need to do between now and then, to be able to feel like that. Initially think about broad ideas. Once you have these fixed in your mind, you can begin to work on the practicalities and fill in the details. You may need to keep refining the details until you are satisfied that they are realistic.

3 Take a blank piece of paper and write your plan down, visualizing exactly how it would look and trying to imagine how it would feel. Work on the details until your plan feels right for you.

4 Work out what you need to change about yourself in order to achieve your dreams. Once you have decided which aspects of your character you want to work on, you can then use feng shui to help bring about a change. For example, if you want to be more playful, you could look at strengthening the chi of the west in your home, or at absorbing more of this chi by turning your bed so that the top of your head points to the west.

WATER FEATURES

WHAT Fountains, aquariums and other water features
BENEFIT Improves your health, brings more vitality into your home
HOW TO USE Place in the east or south-east of your home or room
SOURCES Available from specialist shops, household stores and garden centres

DID YOU KNOW?

People have traditionally gone to the sea, spas or springs to heal injuries and recover from illness. This explains the feng shui principle that the chi of fresh, clean water has a positive influence on the water chi in your body.

The human body is essentially made up of water, and the chi of the water inside your body has a similar frequency to the chi of any water nearby, making it possible to create a powerful connection between the two. If the chi of the water outside your body is pure and clear, while the chi of the water inside your body is weak, then the outer chi can improve the strength of your inner chi.

You can bring water features into your home by adding small indoor waterfalls, fountains, aquariums or simply a bowl of fresh water that is refilled daily. Moving water will add more yang, vibrant energy; still water will add more yin, calming energy. To gain its beneficial effect, the water must be clean and fresh, so change it frequently.

SEA SALT

WHAT Sea salt – fine or coarse grains
BENEFIT Improves stability and purifies chi
HOW TO USE Place in the north-east or south-west of your home, or sprinkle over the floor
SOURCES Available from health-food shops and most supermarkets

Sea salt is helpful for cleansing chi and stabilizing the flow of chi through your home. It connects to the salt in your blood, sweat and tears, potentially having a powerful influence on your inner chi. The salt will draw in chi from the room, taking away with it any stagnant, stale chi. Put two tablespoons of sea salt in small ramekin dishes, and place these in the north-east and south-west parts of your home. Alternatively, sprinkle some sea salt on the floor before you go to bed, and vacuum it up the next day or throw it out of your home. The salt in the ramekins needs changing every two months.

DID YOU KNOW?

Humans have a strong evolutionary connection to salt, from the time when we lived in the sea. Most of our body fluids have a salty taste. Try putting a small sachet of sea salt over your navel or in the waistband of your trousers, in order to feel more secure.

PLANTS

WHAT Any kind of indoor plant
BENEFIT Helps bring living chi into a space and reduces air pollution and noise
HOW TO USE Grow a variety of plants throughout your home
SOURCES Available from plant shops, garden centres and household shops

Any living thing will bring more natural chi into your home, and one of the best ways to do this is with plants. This is important, as modern buildings can be deficient in chi, due to their insulation materials and the extensive use of synthetics, which often inhibit the flow of chi into a home. A variety of plants is ideal. In general, plants are considered to have wood chi and they are suitable for all rooms as long as they remain healthy. Wherever you are short of floor space, use hanging plants.

DID YOU KNOW?

Grow plants with pointed leaves in corners to help stimulate potentially stagnant chi. Place bushy plants in front of protruding corners, to calm and slow the fast, swirling chi generated by the sharp edges. Grow as many plants as possible in your bathroom, as their wood chi helps soak up any excess water chi.

FLOWERS

> **WHAT** Cut-flower arrangements, flowering plants
> **BENEFIT** Helps change the mood of a space and bring in living chi
> **HOW TO USE** Place fresh flowers in a room where you want to make
> the chi more active
> **SOURCES** Your garden, florists' shops and markets

Flowers bring more colour into your home and as they radiate living chi, their colour has a strong presence. You can vary the mood of a room simply by changing the flower arrangement there. Brighter colours create a more lively, yang atmosphere, and pale shades a more relaxed, yin feel. Flowers radiate more of the chi associated with their colour and direction (see page 36). Since flowers radiate living chi, change the water daily and discard any flowers that begin to wilt. Flowering plants have a similar influence, with the advantage of lasting longer.

DID YOU KNOW?

A vase can also alter the chi of a space. Use rounded metal containers to increase metal chi; glass vases for water chi; tall wooden pots for wood chi; triangular glazed vessels for fire chi; and low clay pots for soil chi.

CLOCKS

WHAT Pendulum clock with as many metal parts as possible
BENEFIT Feeling more organized and having a more structured life
HOW TO USE Place in the west or north-west segments of your home
SOURCES Available from jewellers, household stores and antique shops

Clocks are excellent for adding rhythm to a space, and you can tune into this, making it easier to find your own rhythm. Clocks bring in more yang chi and are associated with metal chi in the five elements. Place them in the

west or north-west segments of your home to strengthen the metal chi there, or in the north part of your house to support the northern water chi.

DID YOU KNOW?

If you fill a room with pendulum clocks, they will all swing together after a while. Any rhythmic cycle encourages other cycles with a similar rhythm to synchronize. For example, women living together often find that their menstrual cycles harmonize. The rhythmic motion of a pendulum and its ticking sound will fill your home with a rhythm that you can tune into to. You are made up of rhythms (heartbeat, breathing), so the rhythms of life make a big difference to the way you feel.

CHARCOAL

> **WHAT** Sticks of artists' charcoal
> **BENEFIT** Ensures harmony when fire chi is in the west or north-west
> **HOW TO USE** Place the charcoal in a clay pot and put close to the source of fire chi
> **SOURCES** Available from art supply shops

Artists' charcoal generates a strong soil chi. It is left over from wood that has been burnt and cooled, and mirrors the five-element cycle of wood, fire, soil. Any strong fire chi could have a destructive effect on the metal chi of the west and north-west parts of your home, if there is insufficient soil chi. Use charcoal to help harmonize the energy when you have a fireplace, cooker, boiler or oven in the west or north-west of your home.

DID YOU KNOW?

The matt-black porous surface of charcoal means that it readily absorbs chi and can therefore be helpful wherever you want to pull the chi down. Try putting the charcoal near a southern door or in the south of your home, if you feel over-emotional or find that you have frequent unnecessary arguments.

CANDLES

WHAT Wax candles

BENEFIT Helps you feel fiery, passionate and intimate

HOW TO USE Light candles in the south, south-west and north-east parts of your home

SOURCES Available from specialist and household stores

DID YOU KNOW?

You can use a candle to help you meditate and to empty your mind of busy chi. Light a single candle and sit so that you face north, with the candle at the same height as your eyes. Look into the flame and focus on the process of wax transforming itself from a solid to a molten liquid, into a gas, and finally into light and heat. As you fully absorb yourself with this observation, breathing slowly and deeply, you will allow the peripheral chattering chi to float away from you, as the chi of the candle floats into the atmosphere.

Candles add more fiery energy to a space, although they are softer and more yin than electric lighting. The fire chi of candles strengthens the fiery chi of the south and supports the soil chi of the south-west and north-east. Keep them in pairs if you want to improve or start a relationship. You need to light the candles for them to have any influence on the chi around them.

MIRRORS

WHAT Flat or convex mirrors
BENEFIT Creates a faster, more exciting, spacious, active environment
HOW TO USE Hang in dark or narrow rooms
SOURCES Available from specialist shops and household stores

Mirrors help redirect chi and keep it moving. They are ideal in rooms that are dark, because they reflect the available light and chi back into the room. In small or narrow rooms, large mirrors give the impression that the room is wider than it actually is. Hang the mirrors on the longer walls, to create the impression that the proportions of the room are closer to a square. Mirrors are associated with water chi.

Avoid positioning mirrors so that they are directly opposite a door or window, as they will reflect the chi back out of your home again. Two mirrors opposite each other risk chi bouncing back and forth, creating a more frantic atmosphere. Keep mirrors in your bedroom to a minimum.

DID YOU KNOW?

Convex mirrors are round, fish-eye ones that help disperse chi energy. Use them where your stairs lead straight to your front door, or in a long corridor.

WIND CHIMES

WHAT Metal or wooden wind chimes
BENEFIT Disperses chi, leading to a more even and relaxed environment
HOW TO USE Hang by a door, so that the chime is hit each time the door is opened
SOURCES Available from specialist shops and garden centres

DID YOU KNOW?

Wind chimes are only active in terms of feng shui when they chime, so if they do not ring because they are above a door or out of the wind, you need to ring them yourself frequently.

The sound of a wind chime sends out ripples of energy, which help to move and spread out chi. Chimes can also disperse concentrated chi, making it more yin. You can therefore spread out the chi that is rushing through your entrance, helping to fill your whole home with new chi.

The sound of metal wind chimes radiates more metal chi; such chimes are best in the south-west, north-east, centre, west, north-west and north areas, where metal chi is harmonious with the ambient chi. Use wooden wind chimes in the east, south-east and south parts of your home, where the wood is harmonious with the wood and fire chi.

CRYSTALS

WHAT A spherical multi-faceted crystal, which should come with a cord attached

BENEFIT Brings more natural sunny, yang chi into a dark room

HOW TO USE Hang in a window so that it will catch some sunlight

SOURCES Available from specialist shops

DID YOU KNOW?

You can spin a crystal gently to create a more dynamic, yang effect. However, you can confuse the flow of chi if you have more than one crystal in a room.

Crystals refract sunlight into the colours of the rainbow and spread this chi around the room. In terms of the five elements, crystals relate to water chi, so place them in the west, north-west, north, east and south-east parts of your home, to be harmonious with the ambient chi in these areas.

SPACE-CLEARING

WHAT Meditation
BENEFIT Charges the atmosphere of your home with your own chi
HOW TO USE Sit and meditate on the positive thoughts you want to project into the room
SOURCES Yourself

Your thoughts and emotions radiate from your body and mix with the chi energy of your home. To surround yourself with the kind of energy that helps you live the way you want to live, you need to put more of that particular energy into your home. One way to do this is to meditate and focus your mind strongly on what you are trying to achieve. Each time you breathe out, imagine you are breathing those thoughts out into the room.

DID YOU KNOW?

Chanting or clapping as you breathe out and project your thoughts makes the process more powerful, as the sounds carry the chi into the far corners of your home.

BELLS

> **WHAT** Small hand bell
> **BENEFIT** Helps you send out feelings or thoughts with strong chi
> **HOW TO USE** Hold close to your body and ring strongly
> **SOURCES** Buddhist suppliers, catalogues and shops

The sound of a bell helps to distribute chi and send it out to any part of your home where you can hear the sound, as the sound waves carry chi with them. Ringing a bell is particularly helpful for sending your own chi out further.

Hold the bell close to you when you ring it, so that the sound originates from within your superficial chi. Live the dreams you want to project in your mind as you ring the bell. As you ring it, the sound waves ripple through your outer chi field and into your home, carrying your chi energy with it. Keep a hand bell with you and ring it whenever you have a thought or feeling that you want to send out strongly.

DID YOU KNOW?

Hand bells are also useful for stirring up stagnant energy. If your home is feeling flat, take a hand bell and ring it in all the corners and anywhere that dust usually collects. The sound waves will help to get the energy moving again and will encourage fresh chi energy into those areas.

HOW TO USE FENG SHUI REMEDIES: AN EXAMPLE

Take the example of a woman who wants to start a new relationship, but has been single for several years. The aim is to find why she has not been successful, and then create the remedies.

1 Ask:
• Does she meet people?
• Does she go out enough?
• Does she go to right places?

2 Ask:
• Is she too selective?
• Does she feel shy?
• Does she overwhelm potential lovers?

3 Ask:
• Is she too assertive?
• Does she look for commitment too quickly?
• Is she too aloof and gives off the wrong signals?

Making any change with feng shui starts with you. The better you know what you want and what you need to change about yourself to achieve it, the more successful you will be.

4 Find the most likely reason for her difficulty in starting a relationship from her answers to the questions. In this example, let's assume the woman is shy and, even though men she likes are attracted to her, she appears aloof and disinterested. The remedy would be to help her feel more confident, assertive and expressive.

5 Look through the nine types of chi on page 36, to find the ones that will best help. In this example, bringing more eastern and southern chi into the woman's chi energy field would be beneficial.

6 See if it is possible to turn the bed, so that the top of the head points in a more desirable direction, enabling more of that chi to be absorbed. In this case, east or south would be best. If the woman is a light sleeper, south could be too fiery – in which case east would be better.

7 Look in the relevant sectors of the home to see if there are any features there that could be contributing to the problem. In this example, a bathroom in the south (where the water chi could destroy the fire chi of the south, in the absence of any wood chi) needs attention. Eastern or southern chi could be missing from the home's floor plan (depending on its shape), or there might be a lack of chi in the east or south, due to an absence of windows.

8 Introduce remedies. The easiest approach is to add more of the same chi to each area. Here plants, tall wooden features and the colour green would strengthen the chi of the east. Candles, star shapes and the colour purple would strengthen the chi of the south. In addition, you can use the five-elements theory (see page 30) to help. Place plants in a southerly bathroom to make sure there is sufficient wood chi; place a water feature in the east, as water chi supports the wood chi of the east.

THE FENG SHUI
DIRECTORY

MAKE FENG SHUI WORK FOR YOU

This is where you begin to use all the principles of feng shui to help solve real-life problems. Here you will see how to apply design features and remedies (see pages 64–93) to a range of situations that are common to many people.

The directory starts with the methods for applying feng shui to your home. This means feeling comfortable with looking at floor plans, applying the eight directions, doing your own feng shui survey, and assessing the immediate environment around your home.

The next step is to look at the various ways in which you can help resolve different issues in your life. Drawing on everything you have learnt so far, you will become increasingly comfortable with the principles of feng shui as

you apply them over and over again in different situations. The directory is divided into sections on your health, moods, relationships, creativity, finances, family life, career and spiritual life. In addition, there are special sections on moving home (possibly one of the biggest influences on your life, in terms of feng shui) and becoming better connected with nature – a challenge for so many of us as the modern world moves forward.

You can home in on the issues that matter most to you – and try out feng shui for real. The directory also becomes an invaluable resource when you want to help friends and family with feng shui.

The next few pages are all about making feng shui personal to you. As feng shui is simply one way of looking at the universe, and not necessarily the only reality, it is important to take it into your heart and mind in a way that makes it yours. Feng shui needs to work for you and give you the room to be creative and intuitive. If you can master the feng shui basics, you will be in a powerful position to invent your own solutions to suit every unique situation that you encounter.

FOCUS ON PEOPLE

Remember: feng shui is all about people (not houses), so the focus needs to be on the people who live in a home, and on their challenges in life. Only do what is necessary – if everything is generally going well, there is no need to stir things up with feng shui.

Keep your focus on the people in the home, their lives and what they want to change rather than getting distracted by the details of their home.

USE FENG SHUI WISELY

Feng shui will be most powerful if you target exactly what you need from it. The key is finding the missing piece, in terms of your life, and then finding the best feng shui cure to bring in the missing chi. Once you have done this, you need to monitor the results to see if your initial choice of remedy has worked. If not, you can repeat the process with another cure until you are satisfied that you have found the ideal remedy.

Everything changes and you need to keep reviewing your life and, if necessary, make changes to the feng shui of your home to support your new aims.

Find your focus

Try this simple thought process to find the focus for your feng shui.

• Meditate on who you are.

• List your strengths.

• Meditate on what you want to be, where you want to go in life and what you want to do along the way.

• Write down the key points that stick in your mind.

• Try to match your strengths with what you want to be and do, and make a note of any part of you that you need to develop in order to assist your journey through life.

The above process should become your guide to using the rest of this book. The aim is to develop a list of areas to work on, to enable you to be more powerful in your quest to live life to the full. As you progress through life, you will find that your aims and your means of getting there change. It is therefore important to go through this meditation exercise regularly to keep it up to date.

Find the section in the directory that most closely relates to the issue you want to improve. Once you have tried bringing new feng shui solutions into your life, you can review their effects on the challenges that concern you. If you feel you are making progress, continue with your chosen feng shui cures. If you feel you have not made the advances you are looking for, move on to another set of feng shui solutions.

The list below will help you work through this process.

Alternatively, choose a set of new activities – one from each section – to help you implement your ideas across the whole spectrum.

• Review the situation after a few weeks of practice.

• If you are making progress: continue.

• If you feel static: choose another remedy.

DIVINATION AND MEDITATION

An alternative method to find what you really need in life is to tap into your inner self – your deepest chi. Here you can use your unconscious self to make the choices for you. You will no longer be distracted by the delusions that surround you, but will have the clarity and openness to embrace a new line of thought. For example, it may not be wealth, lovers or security that makes you happy after all, but perhaps a spiritual connection, or finding a new way to release your creativity.

You can use divination (selecting a card) or kinesiology (the mechanics of human muscles) to help you. This time get a friend to assist you.

Use cards to tap into your inner chi

1 Take a pack of cards and select eight. Write one of the following words on the inside face of each of the cards, using a marker: health, moods, relationships, creativity, finances, family life, career, spiritual life. Keep these cards separate from the rest of the pack.

2 Turn the eight cards face down. Sit calmly and concentrate on what you want to develop within yourself as you shuffle the cards. Select a card that feels right to you. Turn it over and look at the word on the face of the card. Try the feng shui suggestions in the appropriate part of the directory.

Kinesiology

1 Lie down on your back.

2 Ask your friend to place the eight cards with the words written on them, one at a time, on your body. Place them on your forehead if you want to resolve issues to do with your mind; on your chest for emotional concerns; and on your abdomen for physical ailments.

3 Each time a card is placed on you, try to lift your straight arm up off the floor, while your friend applies firm resistance by holding your wrist.

4 Eliminate the cards where the power in your arm felt weakest. Then repeat the process with the cards that brought out the strongest force, until you have the one card that helps you produce the greatest power in your arm.

5 Go to the appropriate section of the directory and look for ideas that you can apply to your home.

Use a regular pack of cards to make your own divination material.

THE ETHICS OF SACRED FENG SHUI

As you may get involved in helping other people with the feng shui of their homes, and as the relationship between you is important, it is highly desirable to create your own set of ethics, so that you can define that relationship and (if necessary) set boundaries. Clarity on this issue can prevent a lot difficulties later on and get you off to a positive start. This subject is personal to each person who uses feng shui, but here are some suggestion to consider.

Confidentiality

In order for you to reach the source of any problem, the person you are working with will need to be confident that you are someone they can open up to, and that anything they tell you will remain confidential.

Discretion

There is no need to make exaggerated claims for feng shui, or to try and persuade someone else to use it. You will be in a stronger position if you let other people come to you and let your results do the talking. Each situation is unique, and it is very difficult to know to what extent feng shui will have an impact on another person's life.

Focus on issues

Remember that feng shui is all about the person, rather than the building. So even if you find things that could be considered negative about someone's home, but they are not experiencing any problems associated with it, there is no need to worry him or her unnecessarily. Focus on the issues with which the other person has asked for help.

Respect each person's life journey

Everyone has their own journey through life and deserves respect to follow that path as he or she sees fit. Feng shui (and your own role in it) is simply there to help that person with his or her life's adventure. Try not to make judgements or impose your own perception of life on someone else.

Be clear about fees

If there is to be any exchange of money, you need to make it clear what the value of your offering is and what is included in your fee. Write this down, for greater clarity. Make sure there is agreement about what you will provide in terms of ongoing advice.

Set your own limits

There have been cases where feng shui has allegedly been used against another person or business. You will therefore need to decide whether this is something you want to get involved in. If not, make that quite clear to the other party.

Be professional

It can help to set yourself standards of professionalism, in terms of punctuality, keeping accurate records, your appearance, business ethics and the time taken to respond to telephone messages and e-mails.

It is essential to get the relationship right when helping someone else.

FENG SHUI AND YOUR HOME

GET TO KNOW THE ENERGY OF YOUR HOME

This section takes you through the process of putting together all the information you require for your home's feng shui survey. This is where you discover how the chi is flowing through your home. The process goes like this.

1 Create and work with floor plans. Construct a basic map of your home so that you can examine the feng shui of the space.

2 Find the centre of your floor plan. This enables you to accurately align the eight directions over your plan.

3 Take a compass reading and use this to place the eight directions in their correct orientation over your floor plan.

4 Interpret the relationship between the eight directions and your home. This is where you find out which parts of your home could be most useful to you.

5 Look at the shape of your floor plan and use this to see which types of chi are deficient.

6 Discover what kind of chi flows in through the front of your home and the atmosphere this brings with it.

7 Observe the position of the doors and windows of your house or apartment and determine which kind of chi they encourage.

Your floor plans and reading will be referred to throughout the rest of the book as you work through various real-life applications of feng shui.

Most homes are full of synthetic materials. Bring as many plants as possible into your home to create a more balanced environment.

GOOD FENG SHUI PRACTICE

There a some actions that constitute general good practice in feng shui. You should implement these, regardless of the situation.

- *Place a small bowl of sea salt in the north-east and south-west parts of your home, to add greater stability to the flow of chi along this axis.*

- *Fill your home with plenty of plants, to bring in more living chi.*

- *Use natural materials, such as wood, earthenware or cotton, wherever possible so that the chi can flow freely.*

- *Keep your home clean and tidy, and create the space in which chi can move. Too much clutter risks causing stagnation.*

- *Let in fresh air daily to refresh the chi. This keeps a stronger connection with nature, which is all around you.*

WORK WITH FLOOR PLANS

If you do not already have floor plans for your home, you will need to make your own. This is easier than you might think – simply follow the steps below. Basically you are going to put a series of boxes (rectangles) representing each room next to each other on a piece of paper. To decide how big to make each box, you need to measure each room.

USING A COMPUTER

If you are computer-literate you can do the same thing in Microsoft Word or PowerPoint. Simply draw rectangles and put in the dimensions by clicking on 'Size' in the formatting bar. You can then create your own template, with symbols for the windows, doors and items of furniture. This is particularly helpful if you intend to apply this process to several homes, because once you have made your template, it is much quicker to create subsequent floor plans.

How to make a floor plan

1 Use a tape measure to work out the length and width of each room. Alternatively, as the exact scale is not important, you could pace out each room and make a note of how many paces it takes to walk from one end to the other.

2 Think of a convenient scale. For example, 1 pace = 1 cm (½ inch); 1 ft = ¹⁄₁₆ inch; or 1 m = 1 cm.

3 Start with a room in one corner of your home and draw a box on the paper that represents the size of the room, using your scale. You may find it easier to use squared paper so that you can simply count off the squares.

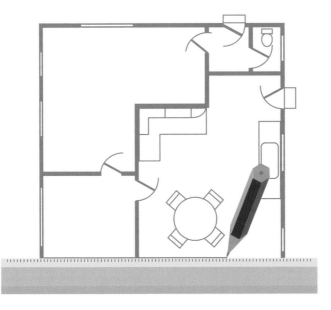

Use a pencil and have an eraser ready as it is easy to make mistakes. Use different coloured pencils for greater clarity.

4 Move on to the next room and draw another rectangle, adjacent to the first. Carry on until you have all the rooms in your home in the correct positions. If your home has more than one floor, you need to do the same thing for each floor.

5 Sketch in all the items that will help you work out where everything is in your home. This might include: windows, doors, stairs, toilets, sinks, baths, showers, dishwasher, washing machine, stove, boiler, fireplace.

6 Cut out 'sticky notes' to represent your furniture, as they will be easy to move around.

FIND THE CENTRE OF YOUR FLOOR PLAN

You need to find the centre of your floor plan in order to position the eight directions accurately. It is used to define which part of your home is east, south-east, south, and so on, so it is important be reasonably accurate. If your home has a complicated shape, you can repeat the process for L-shapes (see opposite) by adding yet another rectangle.

Rectangular homes

1 If your home is rectangular (or close to a rectangle), draw diagonal lines between the corners – the point at which they cross will be the centre.

2 Ignore small extensions, such as a porch, or little indentations in the walls, and draw a rectangle that most closely matches the perimeter of your home.

3 If you live in an apartment, include only the areas that are for your sole use – not any corridors or halls that are shared with people who live in other apartments.

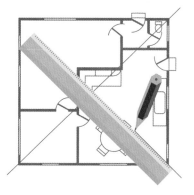

Draw additional lines over your drawing on tracing paper or a photocopy of your original if you are worried about spoiling your floor plan.

L-shaped homes

1 To find the centre when your home has an L-shape, divide your home into two rectangles.

2 Using a light-coloured pencil, draw diagonal lines between the corners of each rectangle to find the centres. Then draw a line between the two centres.

3 Now divide the L-shape into two different rectangles, using another colour.

4 Draw diagonal lines to find the centres of these new rectangles, then draw a line between these two new centres.

5 This new line will cross the line you previously drew (between the centres of your original rectangles): this point marks the centre of the entire L-shape.

6 Wherever possible, fit your L-shape over your floor plan so that you ignore any minor deviations.

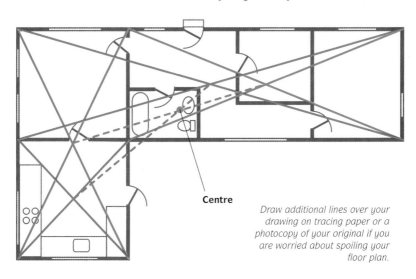

Centre

Draw additional lines over your drawing on tracing paper or a photocopy of your original if you are worried about spoiling your floor plan.

THE EIGHT-DIRECTIONS TRANSPARENCY

This chart will form the basis of your eight-directions transparency (see pages 114–115 for how to apply the transparency to your floor plan). Notice that in this style of feng shui the eight directions are divided into unequal segments. The cardinal points (east, south, west and north) are each made up of 30 degrees, while the remaining directions each occupy 60 degrees. The cardinal directions represent digital changing points in nature:

• **East** Sunrise and the spring equinox
• **South** The sun at its highest point and the summer solstice
• **West** Sunset and the autumn equinox
• **North** Midnight and the winter solstice.

Regardless of the time of year, sunrise and sunset should remain within the 30-degree east and west segments.

To fit into nature's cycle, each cardinal point relates to the appropriate month, so in the Northern Hemisphere east = March, south = June, west = September and north = December (in the Southern Hemisphere, north is associated with the summer solstice and with June; and south with the winter solstice and with December). The changing chi in between is represented by 60 degrees and is associated with two months each.

Copy this diagram onto tracing paper or photocopy it onto an acetate sheet so that you can use it over your floor plans.

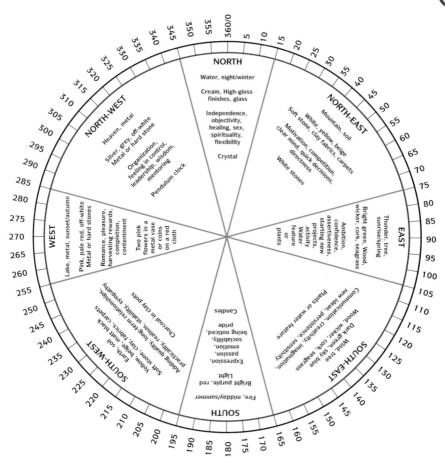

NORTH

Water, night/winter

Cream, High-gloss finishes, glass

Independence, objectivity, healing, sex, spirituality, flexibility

Crystal

NORTH-EAST

Mountain, soil

White, yellow, beige
Soft stone, clay fabrics, carpets

Motivation, competition, clear mind, quick decisions, directness

White stones

EAST

Thunder, tree, sunrise/spring

Bright green, Wood, wicker, cork, seagrass

Ambition, confidence, assertiveness, starting new projects, activity

Water feature or plants

SOUTH-EAST

Wood, wicker, cork, seagrass
Dark green, tree, sky, blue

Communication, creativity, imagination, new ideas, persistence, sensitivity

Plants or water feature

SOUTH

Fire, midday/summer

Bright purple, red
Light

Expression, passion, emotion, sociability, being noticed, pride

Candles

SOUTH-WEST

Earth, soil
Yellow, beige, matt black
Soft stone, clay, fabrics, carpets

Adding quality, long-term relationships, stability, sympathy
Practicality, realism,

Charcoal in clay pots

WEST

Lake, metal, sunset/autumn

Pink, pale red, off-white
Metal or hard stones

Romance, pleasure, harvesting rewards, completion, contentment

Two pink flowers in a metal vase or coins on a red cloth

NORTH-WEST

Heaven, metal

Silver, grey off-white
Metal or hard stone

Organization, feeling in control, leadership, wisdom, mentoring

Pendulum clock

APPLYING THE EIGHT DIRECTIONS

To apply the eight directions, you need to take a compass reading in your home, so that you can orientate the transparency of the eight directions (see page 113).

How to apply the eight directions to your house

1 Stand inside your home and point the body of your compass towards the front wall. Choose the room that has the least electrical equipment and metal items, because they will distort the earth's magnetic field and give you a false reading. To check whether you are getting a true reading, walk around the room holding the compass steady and see if the needle sways. If it does, the field is distorted and you need to choose another part of the room – or another room.

2 Holding the body of your compass so that it faces the front wall of the room, turn the dial and take your reading. Make a note of the reading (for example, 135°), as you will need this later.

3 Photocopy the chart of the four directions (see page 113) onto acetate (this is the kind of transparency used in overhead projectors and is available at most photocopying centres).

4 Cut around the dotted line of the chart. You now have a circular transparency of the eight directions.

5 Next, draw a line on your floor plan, in colour, from the centre of your home straight through the front of your home.

6 Put your eight-directions transparency over your floor plan so that the centre of the transparency lies over the centre of the floor plan. You may find it

best to stick a pin through the transparency and floor plan to keep them in place.

7 Now turn the transparency so that the compass reading you took while facing the front of your home (for example, 135°) is the same as the reading on the transparency where it meets the line running from the centre to the front of your home.

You have now correctly aligned the eight directions and can establish where each direction is in your home. Your transparency tells you the direction, the symbol that describes the trigram, and the element, along with suggestions for colours and materials – which could be applied to flooring, furniture and surfaces – in that part of your home. It also notes what qualities are associated with that part of your home, with suggestions for boosting the energy there.

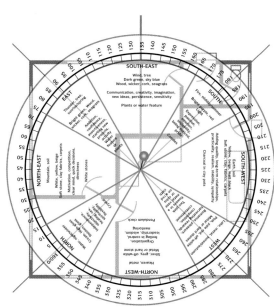

With your feng shui transparency and a compass you can read any floor plan.

READ THE EIGHT DIRECTIONS

Now that you have placed your transparency correctly over your floor plan, you can read off the different types of chi there. Over time the chi will have settled into a pattern, as the daily movement of the sun exerts its influence on your home. Added to this is the influence of the earth's magnetic field, of your own chi and of the chi of the planets in the solar system. The transparency you are using reflects this and helps interpret how it could influence you in your home.

How do you interact with your home?

1 Think about which qualities of the different types of chi are important to you. Read through each of the chi types on your transparency, and locate the direction that could be most helpful to you. For example, being more organized is associated with the chi of the north-west.

2 Look at this direction on the transparency you have laid over your floor plan, and see which part of your home lies beneath it. Consider which room it is, the objects there and how the space is used.

3 Spending more time in that area will make it easier for you to absorb the chi that inhabits that part of your home. Consider whether this is possible and, if so, where you would sit so that you face a helpful direction while being protected by the five animals (see page 34).

4 If it is not possible to spend more time in that area, consider how you can encourage more of that particular chi to spill out into the rest of your home, enabling you to pick it up from other rooms. Look at the appropriate segment on your transparency for ideas on how to increase the chi.

For example, in the north-west you could use an off-white colour, place metal objects there and hang a pendulum clock.

5 Using the five-element theory (see page 30), you can also use elements from the support cycle to enhance a particular chi. For example, the north-west is associated with metal chi, which is supported by soil chi. Soil chi is associated with the south-west, centre and north-east, so any of the colours, materials and objects found in these directions on your transparency would also be effective.

KEY

- ●● Pair of candles
- ● Round-leafed bushy plant or fresh flowers
- ○ Yellow flowers or yellow flowering plant in clay container
- ○ Sea salt
- ● Uplighter
- ● Metal wind chime

- ● Round metal clock
- ● Red or pink flowers in round silver container and some shiny coins on a red cloth
- ● Artist's charcoal in a clay pot
- ● Fresh water
- — Mirror

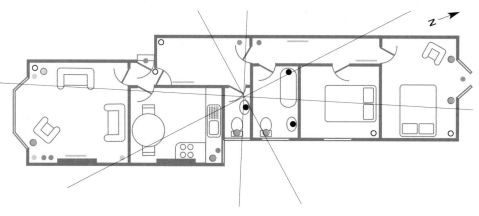

CHECK THE FOOTPRINT

The shape of your floor plan – its footprint – will show you which of the eight types of chi occupies the greatest area in your home and potentially has the greatest influence on your own chi. Other factors are how much and what kind of chi enters through the doors and windows.

If you have a round house, the chi energies will all be distributed evenly. Remember that in this system the cardinal points (north, east, south and west) occupy 30 degrees, while the in-between directions are 60-degree segments, so it is normal for south-east to take up twice the area of east. A square home is also close to even. Long narrow homes, L-shaped footprints and complicated shapes result in some chi directions covering large areas of a home, while other types of chi may not be represented at all on the floor plan.

Establishing a home's footprint

1 Place your eight-direction transparency over the centre of your floor plan and turn it so that it is correctly aligned with north.

2 Look at the different directions and see if they cover the floor plan evenly. Imagine a circle roughly the same size as the footprint, to make a comparison.

3 If all the directions are similar, then your home contains a good balance of all directions of chi. This makes it easier to lead a well-balanced life.

4 If any of the energies are deficient, make a note of them and consult your transparency (or the more comprehensive description of the eight directions on page 36) to see if this lack of chi is affecting your life. For

example, if there is no east on your floor plan, you may lack confidence, self-esteem and ambition, as well as find it harder to start new projects.

5 If you think this the case, you can boost the missing chi by employing the cures shown for that direction on your transparency. Sometimes you will have to put the cures outside your home if the chi is missing completely.

6 If there is no correlation between the deficient chi and your real life, you may find that chi has been compensated for by another means. Then there is no need to provide any remedies.

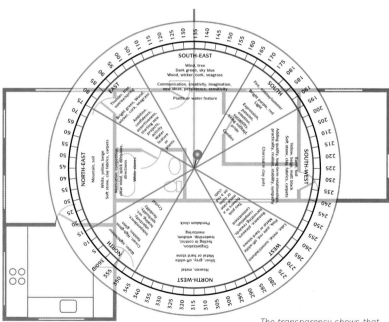

The transparency shows that west, north-west and north chi are deficient in this house.

ESTABLISH THE FACING DIRECTION OF YOUR HOME

The direction in which your home faces will predicate it to draw in more of that chi. This direction is normally the one that faces the entrance to the site and contains your front door. This is clear in a home that faces the road, has a drive leading into the property or has the front door and garage entrance facing a road.

It is less clear in apartments, because the entrance to the apartment is often from an internal hall, corridor or stairwell. In addition, it is possible that no part of the apartment will face the main road. In this case, the side of the apartment that contains the most windows should be considered the front. If there is a choice, where two or more sides have a similar number of windows, the side that faces the same direction as the entrance to the whole building (or the side that faces the road) should be considered the facing direction of your home.

The theory is that movement along a road stirs up the chi there, and this mobile chi then gets directed towards your home as people or vehicles approach it. This means that a greater amount of chi comes into the front of your home, compared with the other directions. The more people who come up to your front door, the greater the flow of chi. This includes postal workers, delivery people, friends, family and yourself.

How to establish the prevailing type of chi

1 Place your transparency on the centre of your floor plan and turn it so that it is correctly aligned with north.

2 Look at the front of your home to see in which direction it faces. This will be the direction that has the line you drew (from the centre of your home to the front) running through it.

3 Read off the qualities of the particular chi that is brought into your home (and look up the description of this type of chi on page 36). These qualities should be the strengths that you experience while living there.

The front door, windows and garage all face the road, making it easy to determine that this is the front the house.

ASSESSING THE CHI THAT ARRIVES THROUGH WINDOWS AND DOORS

Most of the environmental chi enters your home through the doors and windows, although chi will also rise up through the earth and your floor, along with the heaven chi that comes in through the roof. Skylights greatly increase this flow, creating a greater exposure to the mentally and spiritually stimulating chi from the cosmos. This in turn increases the vertical flow of chi, helping you feel more intellectually independent.

Clear windows let in the most light and chi, whilst frosted glass creates a softer, more yin, effect.

The direction of your doors and windows from the centre will define which kind of chi readily enters your home. The larger the door or window, the more chi will flow through it. The more people who use the door, the more chi will be encouraged to flow in and out of the entrance. Windows that are left bare permit the greatest flow of chi. Full, heavy curtains (even when drawn back) slow down chi.

How to calculate the effect of doors and windows

1 Place your transparency over the centre of your floor plan and correctly align it with north.

2 Make a note of the positions of the doors and windows, in terms of which segment of the transparency they lie in.

3 Look up on the transparency the kind of chi that a door or window in that position will bring in (go to page 36 for a fuller description).

4 If you have a choice of entrances, decide which one brings in more of the chi that would most help you in life. Then use that door more often.

5 Hang a wind chime so that it rings each time you open the door, so that you encourage beneficial chi to spread out and penetrate most of your home.

6 See if any of your windows face a direction that would bring in more of the beneficial chi that you think you most need. Ensure this window is kept uncovered as much as possible, and open it daily.

Doors with large windows let chi through more easily when closed.

FENG SHUI AND YOUR HEALTH

A HEALTHY HOME

Ideally, your own chi will flow easily around your body. From an energy perspective, most health problems are created by disturbances in the normal flow of chi. This could occur in areas where the chi in your body is stagnant, compressed, too fast-flowing or deficient. The reverse is also true: any physical ailment will result in a contorted flow of chi.

To help your chi find a healthy flow, it is best to immerse yourself in chi that is flowing freely, gently and harmoniously. This will calm any fast-flowing chi inside you and invigorate any stagnant chi. The aim of this section of the directory is to give you ideas on how to achieve this.

Prime areas for consideration are: your kitchen and larder, as these

influence the chi that you take in; any place where there is water, as this can interact with the ambient chi in a way that has an adverse influence on the water chi in your body; and your bedroom, because this is where you spend most time in one place and where you regenerate.

If you know exactly what kind of chi you need in order to improve your health, you could

This large open room, with no clutter, lets chi move freely.

KEEPING YOUR HOME HEALTHY

In general you will find it easier to maintain good health in a home that:

- *Has exposure to natural light, including some sunlight*

- *Is made from natural materials*

- *Has a variety of plants inside*

- *Is furnished with items made from natural fabrics and materials*

- *Is aired daily*

- *Is in an area where there is clean unpolluted air*

- *Is surrounded by some natural vegetation and trees.*

You may find it harder to maintain good health in a home that:

- *Is close to high-voltage electrical power lines*

- *Is close to a high-voltage electric railway line*

- *Is built on toxic waste ground*

- *Exposes you to strong internal electromagnetic fields*

- *Uses fluorescent lighting*

- *Has synthetic carpets, fabrics or bedding*

- *Is damp, cold or has mildew*

- *Is dark (a basement or north-facing home)*

- *Is close to a busy, high-volume road*

- *Is dirty or dusty.*

recreate that chi in a part of your home where you spend plenty of time. For example, if you need more upward chi, you could sit in the east part of your home, facing east. The effect would be even stronger if you surrounded yourself with tall plants, because they increase the upward direction of chi flow.

KITCHEN AND LARDER

BENEFIT Adds healthy chi to the foods you store, prepare and eat

Your kitchen is the room where you store, prepare and cook your foods, and your larder is where you store foods. During its time in these spaces your food will absorb some of the chi energy already present. It is therefore important that your kitchen contains healthy chi, as you will end up actually eating some of this energy. This could have a subtle influence on your health in the long term, since the process has a cumulative effect. Here are the steps needed to create healthy chi in your kitchen and larder.

What you do

• Make sure the kitchen is easy to clean and free from damp or stagnation.

• Ensure your kitchen is exposed to plenty of natural light and fresh air.

• If you have a choice of rooms, use a room in the east or south-east part of your home so that it is exposed to the rising sun. Here the cooker and sink are both in harmony with the ambient wood chi of these directions, in terms of the five elements. The water of sinks, washing machines or dishwashers is associated with water chi, and the cooker with fire chi, creating the supportive cycle water-wood-fire.

• Choose surfaces such as wood or stone to keep the chi flowing. Wood is softer and therefore more yin and relaxing, whereas stone creates a more yang, pristine atmosphere.

• Avoid fabrics, soft furnishings and carpets, as they absorb damp and smells, increasing the risk of stagnation. These materials make it harder to keep the kitchen clean. Synthetic materials can block the flow of chi and should therefore also be avoided.

• Use a gas cooker so that your food will cook on a natural flame. Electric cookers immerse your food in an electromagnetic field, upsetting the food's natural chi. Microwave ovens subject your food to strong electrical radiation, altering the chi of your ingredients.

Plants will soak up water from the atmosphere making them ideal in any place that might be too damp.

• Use incandescent lighting rather than fluorescent lighting, to help reduce your exposure to electromagnetic radiation. A variety of spotlights, uplighters and diffused lighting controlled by dimmer switches will provide you with the flexibility to create different moods.

• Grow plenty of large leafy plants to add more living energy to your kitchen.

• Organize sufficient storage space to keep all your equipment and food in, so that your work surfaces are clear and free of clutter.

FOODS AND TEAS

BENEFIT Greater absorption of chi

Apart from eating a diet that is complete and well balanced in terms of nutrients, there is great benefit from also thinking in terms of the chi of your food. Everything you eat has its own chi energy field and, once this is inside you, it will have a subtle influence on your own chi. If you continue to eat the same foods over a long period of time, they will start to have a pronounced effect on you.

Concentrating on whole living foods will bring more natural living chi into your body.

What you do

As a general rule, it is helpful to try to eat foods that are still 'living' up to the time you cook them. This includes wholegrains, dried beans, vegetables, fruits, nuts and seeds.

• **Vegetables and fruits** To understand the chi of foods, start with the way they grow. For example, root vegetables (such as carrots) grow downwards into the ground, whereas vegetables that grow along the ground (such as pumpkin) have a more relaxed energy. If you followed this line of thinking and wanted to eat carrots for their strength and their ability to grow past obstacles, you would choose those carrots that have had to bend around stones, rather than straight, even carrots that have been grown in soft soil.

• **Meat and fish** Similarly you can think about the characteristics of the animals you eat. Nervous animals (such as chicken) will pass on this type of chi when you eat them. A fish such as wild salmon will give you the chi to swim against the flow and jump obstacles, whereas squid will help you relax and go with the flow.

• **Cooking methods** In addition to the food itself, think about the way it is prepared. Frying on a high flame will add a lot of fiery chi energy to your ingredients. This energy will enter your own chi field, helping you feel more outgoing and expressive. Conversely, slowly stewing a dish will give you more slow-burning energy.

Tea quickly changes your chi, mixing the water chi of the tea with the water chi of your body.

• **Teas** Teas have been used throughout the ages for anything from digestive disorders to headaches. Hot liquids are quickly absorbed into the bloodstream and tend to soothe your digestive system. As water is the main ingredient of any tea (and, as previously discussed, humans are primarily made up of water), the water chi of the tea interacts very easily with the chi of the water inside you, influencing your health and emotions.

WATER IN YOUR HOME

> **BENEFIT** Keeps your chi pure and clean

The water in your home will improve the chi of the water in your body if it is clean, fresh and pure. If the water close to you is stagnant, polluted or dirty, it could interact with the water chi of your body in a way that makes it less healthy. Wherever there is water, it will help if the room has windows.

HARMONIZING CHI

Ideally water will be situated in the east or south-east part of your home, where the water chi will support the wood chi of the east and south-east. If this cannot be achieved, you can harmonize the chi by bringing in the missing element. For water in the:

- *South, try plants*

- *South-west, put plants in metal containers*

- *West, put plants in clay and metal containers*

- *North, put any plants that will grow here.*

What you do

- Avoid leaving any dirty water in the kitchen sink. Always drain it as soon as you have finished, otherwise the dirty water chi will have a negative influence on the people nearby and on the chi of the food stored close by.

- Check to see if you have any leaks. This can occur unnoticed under baths and sinks, as well as behind dishwashers and washing machines. The risk is that long-term damp set in where the water is stagnant, radiating out stagnant-water chi.

• Check to see if any taps drip. Here again, the water can stagnate, creating cold, damp conditions.

• Clean up and dry out any areas where mildew has set in. This is common in showers, baths, on shower curtains and at the base of windows where condensation runs down. Mildew is extremely stagnant in terms of chi, and this chi could be harmful if you are in poor health.

• Air kitchens and bathrooms regularly to help keep these rooms dry.

• Keep the kitchen as uncluttered as possible, because steam from cooking will condense on objects, making it harder to keep the space dry.

Dry the surfaces and sink after washing up to avoid water chi stagnating in this area.

BATHROOMS

> **BENEFIT** Eliminates old chi

In terms of feng shui health, your bathroom can have one of the biggest influences on the chi energy of your home. This is the place where you wash yourself and eliminate waste products. While these physical processes happen, you also get rid of unwanted chi, and this helps to release old emotions and ideas. You may notice that you feel emotionally refreshed after a shower or skin scrub.

One of the risks is that your old chi energy gets stuck in the bathroom and then seeps into the rest of your home. This could create a feeling of being stuck in your old emotions, and might increase the risk of depression.

What you do

• Avoid fabrics, which tend to absorb moisture and increase the risk of stagnation. For this reason it is much better to have a tiled or wooden floor than a carpet. Likewise, wooden blinds are a better choice than curtains. Hang any towels, rugs or bath mats outside to dry on a regular basis.

Plants will absorb some of the humidity in your bathroom giving the room a more healthy atmosphere.

• Each time you flush the toilet, a relatively large amount of water rushes out of your home. This draws some of the chi out of your house at the same time, temporarily causing the chi of your home to wash back and forth. To reduce this effect it is advisable to keep the lid of your toilet closed while flushing.

• Grow plenty of plants in your bathroom to help steady the chi. If you have a window, open it to air your bathroom every day.

It is important to avoid water chi stagnating in bathrooms.

THINGS TO AVOID IN THE BATHROOM

• *Avoid positioning the lavatory close to the door, since it then becomes easier for the surging effect to influence your whole home.*

• *Avoid surfaces that slow the flow of chi energy, such as carpets, curtains, or thick rugs, as they increase the risk of stagnation and dampness.*

• *Avoid covering the windows in a way that reduces the bathroom's exposure to sunlight. Slatted blinds can ensure that the bathroom benefits from natural light, while providing privacy.*

• *Avoid over-furnishing the bathroom, as this can create a more damp, stagnant atmosphere.*

• *Avoid situations, such as an en-suite bathroom, where the bathroom does not have a door.*

PLANTS

BENEFIT Maintains good health

The living chi that plants radiate can have a positive influence on your own chi and make it easier for you to gain, or maintain, good health. You can simply fill your home with a variety of plants, or try to spend more time close to plants that move your chi in a way that helps you feel good.

Plants with more rigid, strong and pointed leaves (such as a yucca) radiate more dynamic yang chi. Plants with softer, more floppy and rounded leaves generate more relaxing yin chi.

What you do

• A bushy plant in front of a protruding corner will slow the chi that is moving from this sharp edge. The plant should ideally obscure the corner from view.

• Several doors in a straight line, a long corridor, and doors or windows opposite each other encourage chi to speed up. To slow this chi, place

FIVE-ELEMENT CHI

In general, plants are classified as adding wood chi to a space. However, within the full range of plants, some have more of one type of five-element chi. These are listed below.

• *Wood Tall plants in which the leaves point upwards move chi up your body.*

• *Fire Plants with pointed leaves that fan out bring your chi out to the surface.*

• *Soil Low plants whose leaves spread outwards help to settle your chi.*

• *Metal Plants with rounded leaves help to contain your chi.*

• *Water Creeping plants and vines encourage your chi to flow more easily.*

Cacti are associated with fire chi and help energy move more actively.

bushy plants close to the windows or doors and stagger plants along a corridor.

• Stairs that lead down to a front door encourage chi to flow quickly and risk some flowing out of the door, leaving a deficiency of chi in your home. To slow this chi, place a bushy plant between the foot of your stairs and the front door.

• Heavy beams supporting a large weight create a strong downward flow of chi that can be oppressive. Growing plants with strong upward chi under the beam will compensate for this.

• It is most common for chi to stagnate in the corners of a room. Yang, fiery plants with strong, pointed leaves help speed up the movement of chi there.

SLEEPING DIRECTIONS

BENEFIT Absorbs healing chi

When you sleep you are particularly receptive to the chi around you. While you are passive, as well as repairing and regenerating yourself, you draw in more of the chi around you. Most of this chi enters your body through your crown chakra at the top of your head. You can find this chakra by locating the spiral on the top of a baby's head (or the head of anyone with short hair).

The direction in which your crown chakra points when you lie down will determine which of the eight types of chi you will absorb more of.

Turning your bed so that the top of your head points north is ideal, if you have sleeping problems. Northern chi relates to the winter and midnight, which makes it perfect for you if you need to calm down in general. This water chi is helpful for healing and recovering from health problems. This direction is usually too quiet for anyone who needs to be active during the daytime, so only use it when necessary.

What you do

• Use soft materials in your bedroom, such as carpets, rugs or a softwood flooring. Try curtains instead of blinds.

• Check to see if there are any sharp edges pointing at your bed. If so, grow a bushy plant in front of the corner, or hang soft fabric over the sharp edge.

• Keep all doors and window coverings closed at night, to contain the chi and reduce the risk of it flowing too quickly.

• Remove any mirrors and shiny objects, which can make the chi energy buzz around your bedroom and interfere with your sleep. Make sure that mirrors do not point at your bed and cover the mirrors with a cloth while you sleep.

Sleeping close to a corner and under a beam increases the risk of trying to rest in the line of fast-moving chi. Fabrics and plants would slow the chi.

• Try to arrange your bed so that you can see the window and door easily as you lie down, so that the chi of the phoenix is in front of you.

• If you cannot turn your head to point north, try west or north-west, which both help to contain your chi.

BEDS AND BEDDING

BENEFIT Better sleep and health

Beds and beddings are highly influential on your sleep, as they are part of your chi field. The quality of your sleep will greatly affect your long-term health. It is important to get about six hours of deep, undisturbed sleep each night, so that your body can repair, heal and regenerate itself properly.

What you do

Bedframes

• Wood is the ideal material for a bedframe, as it does not distort the local magnetic field. Wood is also softer than metal and attracts a more yin, calming chi into your chi field.

• A four-poster bed helps contain the energy around you and is particularly useful if you sleep in a large bedroom with high ceilings, where the chi energy can move quickly.

Hanging fabric on the wall behind your bed will slow chi around your heads, making it easier to sleep.

• The height of your bed should be in proportion to the height of your ceiling. So in a bedroom with a low ceiling, use a low bed such as a futon on a base. Try to keep at least 1.8 m (6 ft) between the top of your bed and the ceiling so that there is plenty of room for your chi to move freely. The higher the bed, the more you may be stimulated intellectually. The lower the bed, the more practical you should feel.

Mattresses

• Choose a mattress made from natural materials. Cotton, wool, straw and hair are preferable to foam and other manmade materials. Synthetics carry a static charge and, as this will be inside your chi field, it can eventually make you feel unsettled.

• Cotton futons are ideal, as they promote harmonious chi flow. Use a wooden base to raise the futon off the floor and air it properly, or put a futon on any wooden-slatted bed base. Its firmness will help if you suffer from back problems.

• Avoid pocket-sprung mattresses containing metal springs, as they distort the local magnetic field.

Bedding

• It is best to have pure cotton or linen closest to your skin for good chi flow. These materials also breathe, which is important because humans can secrete up to 1 litre (1¾ pt) of fluid at night through the skin while sleeping.

• Avoid synthetic fabrics.

• Avoid using an electric blanket, as it will greatly increase your exposure to the electromagnetic field. Even when the blanket is switched off, it will distort the natural magnetic field.

ELECTROMAGNETIC FIELDS

> **BENEFIT** Physical and emotional well-being

Electromagnetic fields (or EMF) surround anything that uses or transports electricity. Exposure to these fields distorts your own chi, potentially compromising your physical and emotional well-being.

The greater the use of electricity and the closer you are to it, the greater the effect. This includes computers, televisions, microwave ovens, electric cookers, electric heaters, electric blankets, hair dryers, photocopiers and fax machines. The following steps suggest what you can do to reduce your exposure.

PLANTS

Research indicates that plants can help reduce the adverse affects of EMF. The Institut Des Recherches en Geobiologie at Chadonne in Switzerland carried out a two-year research programme in offices on New York's Wall Street, to examine the effect of keeping plants next to computer terminals. The most effective plant was a Cereus peruvianuf *(a type of cactus, 40 cm/16 in high), which reduced the incidence of headaches and tiredness among employees when placed next to the computers. Other investigations have promoted the peace lily and spider plant as having similar properties.*

What you do

• Keep as far away as possible from the source. For example, the difference between being 0.5 m (1½ ft) and 1 m (3 ft) from a computer will be much greater than half.

• Only use electrical equipment when it is really necessary, and avoid leaving it on. It is safest to unplug equipment when it is not in use, so that electricity does not continue to run through the transformer. Often the strongest EMF comes from the transformer.

• If possible, site your transformer at a distance: some equipment (such as a laptop computer) has a remote transformer on a lead, which you can site well away from you, even though the rest of the equipment is closer to hand.

• Set up your workplace so that equipment that emits EMF is as far as possible from you.

• You are at the greatest risk when you are asleep, so it is worth arranging your bedroom to minimize your exposure to EMF. Keep electric alarm clocks, televisions and radios as far from your bed as possible.

• Keep mobile and cordless phones as distant as possible, since the use of them has been associated with brain tumours, memory loss, depression and lack of concentration. At home use a traditional land line.

Keeping a plant close to your computer can slightly reduce your exposure to EMF.

POLLUTION

> **BENEFIT** Improved health

Another risk in a modern home comes from toxic fumes. Some synthetic materials emit toxic fumes for up to ten years after their manufacture. Examples include furniture or built-in units made of medium-density fibreboard (MDF) or any other bonded wood fibres and items made from plastic; and paints. Better modern insulation allows these fumes to build up in your home, increasing their concentration.

In addition, living near a busy road, in a city with heavy traffic or an industrial area may increase your exposure to airborne pollutants, making you more prone to respiratory illnesses.

This room contains many natural materials which will help improve the air quality.

What you do

• Select objects from natural materials, such as wood, metal, pure cotton, leather, china or glass.

• Open the windows every day and thoroughly air your home and workspace.

• When redecorating, use organic paints and varnishes.

• Try waxing wood with natural waxes, instead of using commercial varnishes or lacquers.

• Keep as many plants as possible in your home to help clean the air.

REDUCING AIR AND NOISE POLLUTION

NASA scientists have found that plants are one of the best ways to clean the air. Keep a variety of healthy plants throughout your home to improve its air quality. The top ten most effective plants (in alphabetical order by common name) are:

- *Bamboo palm*
  (Chamaedorea seifrizii)

- *Chinese evergreen*
  (Aglaonema modestum)

- *English ivy*
  (Hedera helix)

- *Gerbera daisy*
  (Gerbera jamesonii)

- *Janet Craig*
  (Dracaena glauca 'Janet Craig')

- *Marginata*
  (Dracaena marginata)

- *Mass cane/corn plant*
  (Dracaena massangeana)

- *Mother-in-law's tongue*
  (Sansevieria trifasciata 'Laurentii')

- *Pot mum*
  (Chrysanthemum morifolium)

- *Peace lily*
  (Spathiphyllum 'Mauna Loa')

Bushy or leafy plants have also been found to be particularly helpful in reducing noise. The leaves absorb the sound waves from the air, making a room quieter and more relaxing.

*Mother-in-law's tongue (*Sansevieria trifasciata *'Laurentii').*

FENG SHUI AND
YOUR MOODS

HOW FENG SHUI CAN CHANGE YOUR MOODS

The most immediate effect that feng shui has is on your moods. Your outer chi acts as an antenna, bringing in new chi, and this will quickly make a difference to the way you think and feel. The following are ways in which you can create different moods in a room. You will find a more detailed explanation of each feature on the pages that follow.

• One of the greatest influences on you are the colours of a space. Walking from one brightly coloured room to another will change your chi, as the different light frequencies pass through your surface chi.

• The imagery and symbolism used in a space can make you feel instantly different, as new thoughts or memories prompted by the imagery change your chi flow.

• Lighting is a quick and flexible way to alter the atmosphere of a room. Flick a switch and bright lighting can change to low, subtle illumination.

• Candles not only produce a softer orange light, but their flickering gives subtle movement to a room. They can have a hypnotic effect, making candles the focal point of a room.

The large windows, size and height of this room encourage chi to move freely, whereas the soft fabrics slow chi, leading to a more harmonious mood.

The high ceiling and skylight encourage a strong vertical flow of chi.

• The proportions of a room define how the chi flows. A tall room makes possible a more vertical passage of chi, encouraging individualism; a low, wide room promotes a horizontal flow of chi, making it easier to connect with other people.

• The kind of furniture you have influences the atmosphere of your home. The shapes, styles and materials it is made of can all have a subtle effect on your emotions. Seating has the greatest influence, because this defines your posture and therefore your chi envelope.

• Real fires give out radiated heat in a similar way to the sun, making them the ideal replacement for sunshine during dark, cold winters. They bring back some of the fiery, sunny chi to your energy field.

• Sharp edges give clear definition to a space, as the chi follows these lines. This can stimulate and define your moods.

• The linear or curved form and shapes of objects mould the way chi ebbs and flows in a room, in turn altering the way your own chi moves. Objects close to you exert the greatest influence.

• Cluttered and empty rooms have a very different feel. Both have their advantages and disadvantages – the key is finding the right balance for you.

COLOURS TO CHANGE YOUR MOOD

BENEFIT Changes and improves your mood

The colours you use in your home have a dramatic affect on its atmosphere. Coloured surfaces reflect certain light frequencies back into the room, filling it with faster or slower frequencies, depending on the colour. These light frequencies go through your outer chi field and change the way your energy moves. As a result, you feel and even think differently.

The brighter the colour, the more yang and active it will make you feel. Bright reds, yellows and oranges are good examples. Pale colours, such as light blues and greens, will help you feel more yin and calm.

What you do

To find out how each colour will make you feel, look at the full description of the eight directions on page 36. Find a direction that has the properties you need more of, and then see which colour is associated with it. Alternatively, use the quick reference chart opposite. For example, if you want to feel more confident and assertive, you need more eastern energy in your chi field. The colour that helps activate this energy is bright green.

Colour applies to fresh flowers, plants, woodwork, pictures, picture frames, pieces of art and furniture, as well as walls, ceilings and flooring.

To make a colour more powerful, you can use it in the same part of your home to which its direction relates. So if you are using bright green, see if you can use it in a room in the east part of your home. Use the eight-directions transparency (see pages 112–115) to see which colours to use.

Colour directions and qualities

COLOUR	DIRECTION	QUALITIES
Cream and translucent glossy finishes	North	Independent, objective, sexual, spiritual
Matt black, brown or beige	South-west	Feeling settled, practical, realistic, intimate
Bright green	East	Ambitious, confident, full of self-esteem, enthusiastic
Dark green or blue	South-east	Creative, imaginative, sensitive, persistent, full of new ideas
Yellow	Centre	Powerful, feeling the centre of attention, having a sense of justice
Silver, grey or off-white	North-west	Feeling in control, dignified, responsible, organized
Rusty red or pink	West	Romantic, focused on the end result, playful, content
Bright white	North-east	Motivated, competitive, quick-witted, sharp-minded
Purple	South	Expressive, passionate, social, emotional

IMAGERY

BENEFIT Triggers positive thoughts

The imagery that you have in your home influences you by triggering certain thought patterns. For example, a photograph of a time when you felt particularly happy can help you recapture some of those feelings each time you see it.

The opposite can also be true: someone living alone who wants to be in a relationship, but keeps a lot of images of single people, and even arranges the objects in their home so that they are on their own, may make it harder to embrace another person in his or her life.

What you do

1 Be sure that the imagery in your home is in keeping with what you want to achieve in life. This includes photographs, paintings and objects. Walk around your home and take a careful look at everything to see if it is really encouraging you. Anything that reminds you of something you are moving away from should be put into storage so that you can see how you feel without it.

2 If being in a relationship is important to you, keeping things in pairs can send out the right message to your unconscious mind. For instance, putting two plants in the same pot symbolizes two living things sharing the same home. Similarly you could have pictures of people together, sculptures of couples in an embrace, and you could arrange objects in pairs.

3 Put pictures of anything that inspires you in your home. If you really want to buy your own home, keep a picture of your dream house on the wall. This will help drive you forward and, if the desire is strong enough, help get you through difficult times. Think clearly about what you want in life, then try to find images as close to this as possible.

4 It is important to put up imagery that reminds you of your past successes. Photographs of happy times, awards or examples of work that you are proud of are all helpful in maintaining your self-esteem and confidence.

The distinctive imagery in this picture could have a powerful influence on you.

LIGHTING

BENEFIT Instant change of mood

Lights generate more yang chi, and this light energy is associated with fire energy. If you have a variety of lights, you can change from bright, stimulating lighting to low, soft lighting at the flick of a switch – an instantaneous way to alter your moods.

There are many different types of lighting:

• Incandescent light bulbs emit a slightly orange light, which helps to create a warm atmosphere so that you feel settled and cosy.

• Lampshades made from fabric or paper soften the light and create a more yin, calming atmosphere.

• Metal or reflective lampshades create a more yang, stimulating atmosphere.

• Spotlamps allow you to focus the light in a particular place and activate the chi in a specific part of your room, creating a more yang, interesting environment there.

• Low-voltage halogen lighting produces a bright, high-intensity light that is ideal for increasing the flow of chi through stagnant places. It also makes very flexible free-standing lighting. Halogen's more yang chi helps you to feel motivated.

• Uplighters are particularly helpful if you have a low or sloping ceiling and want to feel less confined.

• Reflected lighting is useful if you wish to spread and diffuse chi off a ceiling or wall. It makes for a softer, more restful yin atmosphere.

• Table lamps or lights placed on the floor focus your attention downwards, making you feel more settled, cosy and intimate.

• Fluorescent lighting produces a blue hue of light, creating a colder, harsher yang atmosphere.

What you do

1 Place lights in corners to reduce the risk of stagnation there.

2 Position uplighters below beams to reduce the downward flow of chi energy.

3 Direct uplighters onto low or sloping ceilings to make the space feel taller.

4 Use lights in the south, centre, south-west or north-east, when you want to boost the chi of those directions.

5 Hide bright lights behind a plant or paper screen to reduce the glare. This also softens the light, creating a more relaxing, yin atmosphere.

This curved lampshade produces water chi, making an interesting mix with the fiery light source. The soft uneven light makes it easier to feel relaxed and calm.

CANDLES

> **BENEFIT** Increases self-expression

Candles change your mood in two ways. First, they radiate fiery chi into the atmosphere. This is done powerfully, as the fire chi is transported primarily by the light and to a lesser extent by the heat. Second, seeing the wax liquefying, transforming to a gas and combusting is a hypnotic sight. Using candles can be a stimulating experience that makes you feel your emotions more strongly.

Candles are the most yin form of light. They radiate a soft orange light and have the advantage of not generating the EMF of electric lighting. This type of light is ideal when you want to create a soft, romantic atmosphere. In terms of the five elements, candles are associated with fire chi.

Here are some ideas for using candles throughout your home. The candles must be lit in order to have any effect, but make sure that you do not leaving them burning when you are not in the room. Half an hour per day should be sufficient.

What you do

• To feel more expressive, outgoing and social, place a large number of candles in the southern part of your home. This strengthens the southern chi there, helping to change your emotional state.

• To feel more settled and intimate in a relationship, place a couple of candles in the south-west part of your home. The fire chi of the candles supports the soil chi of the south-west, making it easier to realize these feelings.

• To feel more clear-minded and to get interesting insights into your life, try lighting a candle in the north-east part of your home. The fire chi of the

Apart from producing a soft light, candles can be used to warm up essential oils, filling a room with mood-changing scents.

candle supports the soil chi of the north-east. Here you can try meditating as you look into the candle while facing north-east.

• To heighten feelings of romance, try putting a pair of candles in the west part of your home. Place the candles in clay holders so that there is sufficient soil chi to make a harmonious relationship between the fire chi of the candles and the metal chi of the west.

• The sight of fire and water can be very dramatic, and having floating candles in your bath produces this effect. Similarly a water feature with candles is striking and stimulating. To make the elements of fire and water harmonious, bring in wood chi by placing the feature in the east, or by putting the candles in wooden boats.

ROOM PROPORTIONS

> **BENEFIT** Changes the atmosphere

The shape and proportions of a room set the boundaries within which chi energy can most easily flow, even though some chi will still be flowing through the doors, windows and, to a much lesser extent, the walls, ceilings and floors. The height of the ceiling, the size of the room and its layout are all influential on your mood.

What you do

• The size of a room defines how much room there is for chi to flow. The larger the room (particularly if it is sparsely furnished), the more space there is, making it easier for chi to pick up speed. This creates a more stimulating, inspiring environment. A smaller room (especially if over-furnished) slows the flow of chi energy, creating a cosier, more intimate atmosphere.

• A tall space makes it easier for chi to move vertically. This makes you feel connected to the chi energy of the heavens and earth, rather than things to the side of you. In this kind of environment you may find it much easier to ponder big issues, feel mentally stimulated and come up with new original ideas and inspirations.

• A broad space with low ceilings encourages chi to flow horizontally, which helps you feel more connected to the things around you on the same plane. This makes it easier to feel close to people around you. You should find it simpler to communicate with people, share feelings and exchange ideas.

• A square or circular room is more compact and yang in terms of the movement of chi inside, making it an ideal space in which to feel dynamic, functional and alert.

• A circular room reduces the risk of chi energy stagnating in the corners, but increases the risk of chi energy spinning around the room. The result is that a circular room can feel a bit unstable.

The height of this room encourages upward wood chi whilst the pointed ceiling brings in more fire chi.

• A long, thin, rectangular room or a long, oval-shaped room feels more tranquil and yin. This is particularly true of an oval room, where chi energy can flow smoothly, avoiding any corners. These types of room have a more distinct atmosphere, depending on their orientation, as they contain more of some of the eight-directional chi and less of others.

FURNITURE

> **BENEFIT** Changes the way you feel

The most important furniture, in terms of feng shui, are chairs, because they define where and how you sit. The more time you spend in them, and the more important your activities while seated at a particular chair, the greater the incentive to get it right, since this can affect the quality of whatever you do while seated there.

What you do

When choosing any kind of seating, it is worth considering its height.

• A tall stool aligns you with rising wood chi, making it easier to feel alert, active and ambitious, as your posture tends to be more erect. This in turn makes it easier for your chi to rise up through your chakras.

• The higher the ceiling of your room, the more suitable tall furniture becomes.

• Conversely, sitting on the floor on a large cushion exposes you to more settled, soil chi, making it easier to relax, feel closer to someone and be comfortable. Here you can adopt a more slanted pose, encouraging your own chi to align with horizontal chi.

• When you want to combine the seating with a table, and the arrangement is intended for several people, the table defines how you interact, because its shape determines your orientation to each other.

• A round or oval table enables everyone to see each other and interact easily. This is ideal to get everyone involved in the conversation.

• A round table symbolizes metal chi energy and helps contain the energy around the table.

Try to bring in furniture to suit every mood.

FLEXIBILITY

Try to have a variety of furniture so that you have something for every occasion and so that you can create the mood you need at any particular time.

• Long, narrow tables are better when you want to establish someone at the head of the table and give them greater authority. For eating, it is best to adopt a straight posture to aid digestion. Here are some considerations.

• Straight-backed chairs make it easier to keep your digestive organs in alignment while eating, but are less comfortable if you like to spend a long time over your meals.

• Kneeling on the floor around a low table makes it easy to feel grounded and to relax with a straight back.

• Sitting on stools around a counter is ideal for quick snacks, while still maintaining your correct posture.

FIREPLACES

BENEFIT Creates a warmer mood

Rather like the sun, a fireplace adds not only convected heat, but also radiated heat – something central heating does not do. For this reason a fireplace can greatly enhance the comfortable atmosphere of a home during the winter, especially if you live far from the equator and have limited hours of sunlight. In addition, a fire provides yang fire chi, which helps you feel passionate, spontaneous and expressive. If you are prone to feeling depressed during the winter months, a real fire can help to replace some of the chi that you may be lacking. It is common to hang a mirror over a fireplace, and this has the effect of reflecting even more of the fire chi into the room.

What you do

If your fireplace is located in a position that does not mix with the five-element chi of that location, you can use feng shui remedies to harmonize the flow of chi. In the following areas your fireplace may not mix harmoniously with the surrounding chi, but some suggested remedies are given.

• **Fireplace in the south** If you are prone to feeling over-emotional, you may need to subdue the fire chi, as the fireplace adds to the fiery chi of the south. A low clay pot filled with charcoal will have this effect. Matt black is associated with the south-west and this colour will further drain the fire chi.

• **Fireplace in the west or north-west**
To harmonize the fire and metal chi, you need to increase the soil chi. A low clay or china bowl filled with charcoal and the colour black will help.

• **Fireplace in the north** To harmonize the fire chi with the water chi of the north, you need to increase the presence of wood chi. This can be done by growing tall plants within a safe distance of the fire, by using the colour green or by putting tall wooden ornaments above the fireplace.

• **Fireplace in the south-west or north-east** A fireplace in these directions will be in harmony with the ambient chi, as fire supports soil chi.

The fire chi, heat and glow from a fireplace can become a focal point in a room and often defines the layout of seating.

SOFTENING SHARP EDGES

BENEFIT Feeling more settled

Any corner that points into a room will direct fast-flowing chi, which can be a problem if it funnels the energy towards somewhere you sleep or relax, resulting in you feeling unsettled, on edge and tense. Fortunately, the remedy to sharp edges is simply to put something soft in front of them, to slow and damp down the fast-moving chi.

What you do

1 Check all the places where you sleep and relax to see if there are any corners pointing at you. Tall corners or long edges, such as a sharp beam, are of most concern because they direct a significant amount of chi; the corner of a table, on the other hand, will not have as great an effect.

OTHER BUILDINGS

Your entire home could be subjected to fast-flowing chi if the corner of another building points towards you, making your house a less relaxing place. The remedy is to plant bushes and trees between the corner of the building and your home. In addition, you could put something convex and reflective on the outside of your home, pointing back at the offending corner. This could be a small convex mirror or a shiny metal plate, to direct some of the fast-flowing chi away from your home.

This corner could be softened by growing a plant in front of it.

2 Make the corners softer. The easiest way to do this is to put a plant in front of the corner. The plant will soften the edge and protect you from any fast-flowing energy. In addition, the plant has its own living chi field, which will make it harder for the fast-flowing energy from the corner to pass through. In situations where you cannot have a plant standing on the floor, try using a hanging plant so that the plant trails down in front of the corner.

3 If you cannot use a plant, hang a fabric ribbon or drape a cloth in front of the corner to soften it. Alternatively, you may be able to put a screen in front of the sharp edge.

4 If you are having a new home built or renovated, get the protruding corners rounded off and avoid the problem altogether. You only need to get a round corner similar to the radius of a coffee mug to make your whole home feel softer and more harmonious.

LINEAR VERSUS CURVED FORMS

BENEFIT Creates a harmonious mood

Rooms that are arranged in long, straight lines with sharp corners create a functional, yang atmosphere in which everything is clearly laid out. However, this is at odds with the natural curves found in nature and in the human body, making it harder to feel connected and in harmony with the room. This might be helpful in rooms where you want to be functional and get things done (such as a kitchen, utility room or storage space), but you may feel too yang and agitated if it affects a room you want to relax in.

The yin curve of this chair subtly breaks up the more yang straight lines of the floor boards.

What you do

1 Wherever possible, include subtle curves in the design of your furniture and fittings, to create a more interesting appearance. The furniture should all have rounded corners and be an oval or round shape, to reduce cutting chi and more closely mirror the shape of your body.

2 Where this is not possible, include artwork that carries natural forms found in nature. Still-lifes, landscapes and portraits will create this imagery.

3 Use objects that carry the human form. This can most easily be achieved with sculptures of people. If this is your choice, try to find poses in which the subjects are expressing something that you aspire to.

4 Use fabrics such as pulled-back curtains to bring a softer flowing line into your room, making it easier to feel in harmony with the space.

5 Try using patterns that contain curves to bring greater harmony to a room you want to relax in. This might be circles, wavy lines or random abstract images.

6 If you are redecorating, consider using special effects, including rag rolling, coarse brushing, sponging or stamping, to get that random mottled effect so often seen in nature.

7 Use living examples from nature, such as plants and flowers, to give your room that humanistic, natural mood.

GETTING THE FURNITURE BALANCE RIGHT

BENEFIT Achieves the necessary balance to create the mood you desire

The more furniture you put in a room, the slower the chi will flow. If the furniture is soft and textured, the chi will move even slower. This makes for a very comfortable, settled mood in which you can relax and feel cosy. The reverse is true of an empty, minimalist Zen room, where the chi will flow more quickly and freely. Here you will find it easier to be in the mood to do things, think about big ideas and be physically active.

What you do

1 Think about how you feel in room. If you find it hard to feel settled and relaxed, you may need to bring in more soft furnishings. To feel more dynamic and energetic, you could try taking things out of the room.

2 To slow the chi and create a more yin mood, bring in items like large cushions, full-length curtains, low plump chairs and big beanbags. Bring in more plants (especially bushy varieties), throw rugs on the floor and try putting lamps with cloth shades on low tables or on the floor. You could even try fabric wall hangings and sheepskin rugs, if you need to take more drastic action to get the chi to slow sufficiently for the mood you desire.

3 To speed up the flow of chi and induce a more yang mood, take items out of the room. Soft-textured objects are most likely to

slow the chi, so look for things that you do not use that can be dispensed with. Chi needs space in order to move, so clear an area in the centre of your room. This should be free of coffee tables and other objects. Take a careful look and remove anything you no longer need. Keep removing items until you feel you have achieved the correct balance.

These soft fabrics slow chi making it move around the chair slowly.

The leather chairs, open space, large windows, lack of clutter and hard surfaces make this an exciting yang space.

FENG SHUI AND
YOUR RELATIONSHIPS

MIX YOUR OWN CHI WITH YOUR LOVER'S

A good relationship is all about being able to mix your own chi with your lover's in a way that makes both of you feel better. The idea is that, as you spend time together, your chi will interact with your lover's, so that you both take in a part of each other. This will happen most actively during sex, when both of you are active and experiencing strong emotions to release to each other. However, simply sleeping together will mean that your chi fields mix in such a way that a little part of your lover's emotional energy is inside you for the rest of the day. Feng Shui aims to make this interaction positive.

• Each of the directions in your home relates to an aspect of your relationship, so you can fine-tune the chi of your relationship by activating a specific direction.

• When you compare the chi of your nine numbers in terms of the five elements, you can see whether you need to add more of another element to your home, to allow for an easier exchange of chi between you.

• The direction in which the tops of your heads point while sleeping helps you absorb a particular chi overnight – the direction determines what kind of chi this is and how it influences your relationship.

• You can set up a particular room, such as your bedroom, for love and sex and create the right atmosphere to make it special.

• In a long-term relationship you may reach the stage where you are happy just to make the most of what you have. If so, you can set up your home to help you achieve this.

• It is possible to mix your own chi with your lover's simply by putting personal things close to each other.

• You can take in similar chi by sleeping, eating and sitting together, giving you both the feeling that you have more in common.

• Flowers are a colourful way to bring more chi into a relationship.

• You can use your year number to work out the best time to start a relationship, get married or conceive.

• You can set up your home so that you find it easier to attract potential new lovers.

• When a relationship ends, you can use feng shui to help you move on and reduce some of the pain.

When you sleep close together your chi energy fields merge, helping you feel closer to your lover.

USE FENG SHUI TO FINE-TUNE YOUR RELATIONSHIP

BENEFIT Enhances your relationship

Each direction and the centre of your home has a special influence on your relationship. This means that you can fine-tune your relationship by making changes to different parts of your home.

What you do

1 Talk to your lover and decide what it is about your relationship that you want to improve.

2 Look at the chart opposite to see which direction is most helpful.

3 Locate the appropriate direction on your floor plan, using your eight-directions transparency (see pages 112–115), and then strengthen the chi there. Use the suggestions written on the transparency to improve the chi in that space.

4 Explore the option of turning your bed so that the tops of your heads point in the direction that best suits your desires.

You can use feng shui to bring about a change in your relationship.

Directional qualities

- **East** Brings more enthusiasm and activity into your relationship. This is helpful when you feel stuck, stagnant or bored in a relationship.
- **South-east** Encourages better communication. This chi makes it easier to sit down and work through any problems.
- **South** Adds more passion and emotion to a relationship. Use this chi when you want more spontaneity and excitement.
- **South-west** Brings in more caring, nourishing feelings. Ideal for creating a secure relationship, with the emphasis on the quality of the way you interact and your companionship.
- **West** Helps you absorb more romantic, playful chi. This makes it easier to

have fun and enjoy the pleasures of being together.

- **North-west** Makes it easier to make commitments and plan ahead. Use this chi when you want to put your relationship on a stronger long-term footing.
- **North** Encourages affection and sexual vitality. This makes it easier to explore the deeper side of your relationship and is ideal for conception.
- **North-east** Improves your ability to be clear, direct and decisive. Use this chi when you want to bring everything out into the open and move forward.
- **Centre** Increases mutual attraction and strengthens the bond between you. Activate this chi to bring you both closer together.

CONSTRUCT YOUR RELATIONSHIP CHART

BENEFIT Creates better harmony

You can use your three ki numbers to try and predict how your own chi will mix with your lover's. One way to approach this is to look at the element that is associated with each of the numbers, and see how they relate to each other.

The same elements

A relationship between people with the same chi helps you understand each other better and potentially reach a closer relationship. It may feel as if you have found your soulmate. The risk is that this kind of relationship could become too stagnant, as you know each other too well.

Harmonious elements

A relationship between people whose elements are next to each other in the five-element cycle is potentially harmonious and supportive. People often naturally find they are attracted to others who either support or calm their energy. Although there are differences between them, these simply add interest and movement to your relationship.

Opposite elements

A relationship between people with elements that are opposite each other in the five-element cycle will be different and exciting. In these relationships there can be great attraction, although it is harder to understand the other person. Such relationships work best when you both respect and enjoy the differences.

What you do

1 Look up your own and your lover's three ki numbers in the chart on page 44–49.

2 Write down your three numbers and your lover's three numbers.

3 Above each of your numbers write the associated element.
1 = water
2, 5 and 8 = soil
3 and 4 = wood
6 and 7 = metal
9 = fire

Then write the elements for your lover below his or her numbers.

4 Compare the elements with the chart given below. Your year numbers apply to the deepest aspects of your relationship and how your lives will interact in the long term. Your month number is initially the most important, as this defines how your emotional chi will mix. Your axis number reveals how your superficial chi combines – this is most useful when you are doing things together.

ELEMENT COMPATIBILITY

Water-water = same

Water-wood = harmonious

Water-fire = opposite

Water-soil = opposite

Water-metal = harmonious

Wood-wood = same

Wood-fire = harmonious

Wood-soil = opposite

Wood-metal = opposite

Fire-fire = same

Fire-soil = harmonious

Fire-metal = opposite

Soil-soil = same

Soil-metal = harmonious

Metal-metal = same

BRING MORE OF THE MISSING CHI INTO YOUR HOME

> **BENEFIT** Encourages chi to move more freely between two people

You can try different remedies to enhance the flow of chi between you and your lover and introduce any missing chi.

What you do

1 Look at the chart below and find the year and month elements for you and your lover (see pages 176–177).

2 Try the suggested remedies and see if your relationship changes.

ELEMENT REMEDIES

 Water-water Try metal energy in the form of pink; or sleep with your heads pointing west or north-west to bring you closer together.

 Water-wood If the person with water chi feels tired, wear pink, red or grey; sleep with your heads pointing west or north-west.

 Water-fire Try sleeping with the tops of your heads pointing east or south-east; grow more indoor plants and use more green to harmonize the chi.

 Water-soil For greater financial security, sleep with the tops of your heads pointing west or north-west; use pink, silver or grey to bring greater harmony.

Water-metal Sleep with the tops of your heads pointing west or north-west; use pink, silver or grey for greater support.

 Wood-wood Add more quiet water chi using cream, and a water feature in the east or south-east to boost the relationship chi.

 Wood-fire Sleep with the tops of your heads pointing east or south-east; grow plants and use the colour green to add strength.

 Wood-soil Place candles in the south; use purple and be sociable to boost the fire chi and create greater harmony.

 Wood-metal An active sex life will bring water chi, as will sleeping with your heads pointing north, bridging the difference in these opposite elements.

 Fire-fire Use soil chi for calming influence: sleep with the top of your heads pointing south-west, or use yellow flowers in clay pot.

 Fire-soil Fire chi brings greater excitement and spontaneity, so try candles in the south; soil chi brings security and stability, so try charcoal in the south-west.

 Fire-metal Use soil energy, in the form of a close family life, along with sleeping with your heads pointing south-west; use yellow to bring greater harmony.

 Soil-soil Add more fire in the form of purple, candles in the south, and an active social life to avoid the risk of boredom and stagnation.

 Soil-metal Absorb more soil chi by sleeping with the tops of your heads pointing south-west and using more yellow in your home.

 Metal-metal Soil chi will help make this a more intimate long-term relationship; try sleeping with your heads pointing south-west and using yellow.

SLEEPING DIRECTIONS FOR ROMANCE, PASSION AND SEX

> **BENEFIT** Feeling more romantic, passionate or sexual

If both of you feel that you are lacking something in your relationship, then you can look through the qualities for each direction (see page 178–179) and use more of a particular kind of chi. The easiest, cheapest and potentially most powerful solution is to turn your bed so that the tops of your heads point in your chosen direction. As you sleep together, you will both absorb more of its particular chi.

What you do

1 Decide what it is that you both need more of in order to enjoy a happier relationship. For example, you might both want a more passionate relationship.

2 Look up which chi would help you most: west for romance, south for passion or north for sex. Check on page 36 to see what other qualities you will be taking in – ideally you should feel happy with the whole package, otherwise you may need to seek an alternative direction.

3 Turn your bed so that the tops of your heads are pointing in the direction of the chi that you want more of.

It is sometimes better to get the direction of your bed right even if you have to position it at an angle. You can make the bed fit the room at an angle using plants, lights and furniture.

COMPROMISE SOLUTIONS

Sometimes facing your chosen direction will not be possible and you will need to select another direction. In this situation, find the direction that is next closest to what you need. If you have a choice of bedrooms, you might be able to achieve your desired direction in another room. Sometime you can temporarily set up your bed in the middle of your bedroom so that it faces your ideal direction. Try it out for a few weeks and, if you notice an improvement in your relationship, explore ways to make the change permanent.

In feng shui it is acceptable for your bed to be set diagonally so that your heads point into a corner, if this means that you sleep in your ideal direction. Fill the empty space with a triangular chest, with plants and flowers on top.

LOVE IN YOUR BEDROOM

BENEFIT Better sex and love life

Intense love and great sex are primarily made up of a feeling that the two of you are almost as one – that your bodies are entwined when moving from one pose to another. Mixed in with this are all the sensations of touch, sight and sound that you take in. These are helped by free-flowing active chi blended with softer, gentle energy.

Candles are softer and more romantic than electric lights, making it easier to pick up on the atmosphere to enjoy a satisfying sex life.

What you do

1 Create the space to move and have the freedom to fully express yourselves sexually. For example, get a large bed, along with big cushions or a comfortable chair, so that you can move to other areas of your room.

2 Think about the lighting. If you enjoy seeing each other, you will need some kind of soft lighting. Candles are ideal as they add more fiery, passionate chi to the room. If you both love the feeling of being close, then a darker room will heighten these sensations.

3 Make the room soundproof enough so that you both feel uninhibited about the noises you make during sex.

4 Create an arousing atmosphere by bringing sexual imagery into your room. This could be sculptures of couples together, paintings or photographs.

5 Orchids act as an aphrodisiac, so a pair of orchids close to your bed can help get you in the right mood.

6 Increase the water, fire and western metal chi, as these help you feel deeply sexual, passionate and playful.

7 To bring more water chi into your bedroom, use cream and a shiny black. Lace and sheer materials will further enhance this. You could also hang a crystal in the north part of your room to empower northern chi.

8 Silk sheets increase fire chi, helping you feel stimulated. Also use bright purple and red in candles to bring in more passion.

9 Pink flowers in a metal vase bring in more playful western chi. The western part of your bedroom is a good place for any sexual imagery.

MAKE THE MOST OF WHAT YOU HAVE

BENEFIT Makes the most of an existing relationship

South-western chi is ideal for making the most of an existing relationship. This chi is associated with the summer changing to autumn and the fruit ripening on the vine. It means taking something you have and making it better. South-western chi helps you feel more caring and like being part of a family unit. Bringing more south-western energy into your chi field will help you both put more energy into your relationship and find ways to improve it.

What you do

1 Bring more south-western chi into your own energy field by turning your bed so that you both sleep with the tops of your heads pointing south-west.

2 Using your floor plan and eight-directions transparency (see page 112–115), locate the south-west part of your home. To activate this chi, place fresh yellow flowers or a yellow flowering plant in an earthenware container in the south-west segment of your home.

3 Use more yellows, browns, beiges and matt black colours throughout your home.

The yellow colour and soft fabrics bring more soil chi into this room strengthening the chi associated with long-term relationships.

4 Support the south-western soil chi with fire chi, by placing a pair of candles in the south-west part of your home. You will need to light them daily for a while to activate the fire chi in this area.

5 Offer ways in which you can both contribute to improving your relationship, while sitting together facing south-west. Focus on what you can do, rather than on trying to change something about your lover. Criticism will simply mean that each of you becomes entrenched in your own position. Listen to each other and really hear what the other person is saying, without interrupting with your own comments.

INTIMACY AND FEELING CLOSER

BENEFIT Feeling closer and more intimate

When two people are in a close, loving relationship, the union begins to take on its own chi. A new chi is created that is a mix of your energies. The more time you spend together, the more your chi mixes. Sometimes people behave and feel very differently when they are in a relationship.

When you are physically close, such as sleeping together, your chi fields merge, creating more of this mutual chi. In theory you will pick up each other's thoughts and emotions unconsciously through this process.

One way to feel closer and more intimate is to take something that has your lover's chi and keep this object close to your person, within your chi field. It needs to be something that your lover usually keeps within his or her energy field (such as clothing, a bracelet, necklace or watch), so that it becomes saturated with his or her chi.

What you do

Keeping personal items close to those of your lover helps mix your chi energies.

1 Wear an item of your lover's clothing that contains his or her chi, so that you bring it into your energy field. This can be reassuring if you have to be apart for some time. Traditionally people would take a lock of their lover's hair. This can also speed up the process of getting to know each other and help you both feel more intimate.

2 Keep your toothbrushes, hairbrushes and shoes close together and mix up some of your clothes when storing them, so that both your energies in these items mix. This makes it easier to access that relationship chi when you use them or put them on. This reinforces the feeling of togetherness and the sense that you are sharing your lives.

3 Keep photographs of you both having fun together in a place where you can see them frequently. If it is convenient, put them in the south-west, west or south part of your room or home, to pick up more relationship chi.

EATING, SITTING AND SLEEPING TOGETHER

BENEFIT Mixes your chi and makes you feel more intimate

The more time you spend close to each other, the more your chi mixes together. If you do this too much, however, there is a risk that you will mix your chi to such an extent that you become too similar. You might then lose the excitement that comes from mixing your chi with someone who has recognizably different chi.

If you do not mix your chi enough, you may find you do not have any real connection with your lover and that, when you face challenges, there is not a strong enough bond to keep you together. Eating, sitting and sleeping are functions where you can naturally be close to your lover.

What you do

1 Try sharing meals. If you arrange to have meals at home, you will have more control over your environment and your food. One of the ways you can both have fun and feel closer is by sharing food from the same container. Any dish that you cook in one container – whether a frying pan, wok or casserole – will give you the opportunity to eat from the same pot. This is common in Japanese cuisine, where you can share dishes such as *nabe* using your chopsticks. This is why the traditional family meal was such a good idea, because when everyone sits down together to share the same food and energy, it creates a bonding experience. If everyone eats separately, it can create greater polarity.

2 Cuddle up together while relaxing in the evening. A big sofa, beanbags or cushions on the floor make this easier. Here you can merge your chi fields while reading a book or watching television, if you do not feel like talking.

3 Sleeping together is perhaps the best way to mix your chi. While you sleep you will be more receptive to your lover's chi, and if you are both naked you are in the closest contact.

Eating or drinking the same things helps you take in the same chi, making it slightly easier to find harmony with another person.

FLOWERS

> **BENEFIT** Improves a relationship

Flowers are one way to bring more romantic chi into a relationship. They radiate both their colour and their living chi into a room. In addition, the shape of the flower defines its distinctive chi. One reason why flowers give out romantic chi is because they are the means by which a plant reproduces.

A large arrangement of flowers with strong colours will be the one thing you notice most in a room. They can even have sufficient chi to make a significant difference to the atmosphere of the whole room. The advantage of flowers is that they are easy to change, so you can alter the energy of a room simply by choosing different flowers.

What you do

• Use strong, sunny colours like yellow or purple when you want livelier chi that is conducive to creating greater attraction and being passionate. These fire and soil colours work well in a container made of clay or china.

• Use cream flowers in a glass vase to help access deeper feelings. They introduce more water chi into your room and help you feel more affectionate.

• Put pink or red flowers in the bedroom when you want to feel more romantic. Place two flowers in a silver vase in order to maximize the metal western chi.

• Change the water daily to bring fresh water chi into the room. Cut the stems regularly on the diagonal if you want them to last longer. Remember to discard flowers before they wilt and die, because they will then radiate a decaying chi into your home.

PLANTS AND ARTIFICIAL FLOWERS

Flowering plants can have a similar influence, although they do not give out the same fragile, yin chi as cut flowers. Any kind of artificial flower will not carry living chi energy and therefore does not make a good substitute.

These flowers exude calming water chi. The cream colour and soft petals help create an atmosphere in which it is easier to feel peaceful.

TIMING

BENEFIT Better understanding your relationship

The phase you were each in at the beginning of your relationship sets up patterns that can stay with you for many years. It is therefore interesting to discover what your initial phase was; from this you can see whether it has had a lasting influence. If you are single, you may be just about to come to an excellent phase, so you could wait to start your relationship at a positive time.

Looking back at the phase each of you was in when you started your relationship can help explain the patterns that have set in.

What you do

1 Look at pages 53–57 to work out the timing of the start of your relationship with your lover.

2 Take the start as being when you first began sleeping together or had sex, because this is when your chi mixes most actively.

3 Read the descriptions below of your own phases and your lover's phases. A 'phase' refers to the position of your year number at the

start of your relationship. For instance, if a couple with the year numbers 8 and 2 started a relationship in a year that had 6 in the centre of the chart, the person with the year number 8 would be in the west of the magic square, and in a phase where he or she had more western chi; the person with the year number 2 would be in the north and in a phase where he or she had more northern chi.

Directional phases

• **East** It is easier to feel enthusiastic now, and you will probably enjoy being active and doing things, but you may be distracted, taking your attention away from your lover.

• **South-east** This helps you make a bright harmonious start, which could generate a positive lasting attitude to the relationship.

• **South** This helps you start with passion, excitement and emotion, so that you quickly become deeply entwined. It is ideal for a quick fling, but risks arguments and emotional upsets.

• **South-west** This is better for people who want to start slowly and carefully build up a relationship that will last. It may not be the most exciting time, but it is one in which you feel caring.

• **West** This encourages you to feel more romantic and enjoy the relationship. You will find it easier to devote more time and energy to the relationship.

• **North-west** This is helpful for a mature couple who value responsibility, but it can be a bit too serious.

• **North** This is helpful for an active sex life, but you may feel insecure, vulnerable and too easily dominated.

• **North-east** This is helpful for being direct and clear about your relationship, but could encourage you to fight with your lover.

• **Centre** Here you are in a strong position to attract people into your life, but you may find it hard to decide if this is the relationship for you.

FIND A LOVER

> **BENEFIT** Having a greater choice of potential lovers

Attracting someone into your life can be assisted by the kind of mood you are in. The character you project when you are out in social situations can make all the difference. When you are happy, show a sense of humour and are playful, people will notice you, finding you someone with whom they would want to spend time. To increase your choice of people to start a relationship with, it is helpful if your environment is one that brings this mood out in you.

What you do

1 Increase the presence of western chi – this playful energy is associated with the sunset, the trigram of the lake and harvest time. To build up this chi, use the colour pink. This will be most effective in the western part of your home. Keep pink flowers here (for example, a pair of pink roses).

2 Place a compass on your bed, and turn your bed so that your head points west and your feet face east. Even though your bed may be at a strange angle within your room, sleep there for six weeks and see if you notice any difference.

3 It will also help to make your home slightly more yin, with pastel colours, soft furnishings and curved shapes. Straight lines, sharp corners and an over-regimented furniture layout will make the atmosphere too yang. Use plants and flowers to soften any sharp edges and to break up straight lines.

4 Clothes that include the colours pink or red, silver jewellery and soft fabrics will all surround you with more romantic chi.

5 Hang a mirror in the west so that its back faces an outside wall, as this will activate the flow of western chi.

The colours you wear send a certain type of chi out into other people's energy field, influencing the way he or she responds to you.

WHEN A RELATIONSHIP HAS ENDED

BENEFIT Letting go of an old relationship so that you can move on

When a relationship ends, you still have the chi of that relationship around you and it can be difficult to more on, unless you can clear out the old chi and bring fresh energy into the vacuum that is left.

What you do

• The chi of the east is associated with beginning a new day and with fresh growth in springtime. This chi is ideal for starting a new phase in your life and leaving the past behind you. To increase the chi energy of the east, place an active water feature (such as an indoor fountain) in the east part of your home, along with tall plants. Wearing bright green clothing will further help. And use this colour for decoration and household objects such as cushions. Sleep with the top of your head pointing east for a while.

• Becoming more yang can make it easier to feel that it is the other person's loss, and that you will find a better new relationship. Eat a more yang diet of fish, root vegetables, grains and thick soups. Physical exercise will help you feel stronger: competitive sports, martial arts and vigorous workouts are yang activities. Wear brighter, yang colours such as red, yellow, purple or bright green.

• Keeping your home clean and clutter-free, with open spaces, will encourage chi energy to flow more freely. A thorough springclean will refresh the chi energy, helping to make a new start and clear out some of the old relationship chi. Get rid of or store any items that remind you of your past relationship.

• Regular body scrubs will encourage your own chi energy to move more quickly, making it easier to let go of disappointments and become more yang. Clean clothes and sheets will introduce fresh chi into your own energy field.

Scrubbing your skin stimulates the surface chi and helps get rid of old emotions, leaving space to fill your chi field with something new.

FENG SHUI AND YOUR CREATIVITY

DESIGN YOUR CREATIVE ATMOSPHERE

The chi around your head influences the way the chi flows inside you, having an impact on your ability to be creative. The secret is to find the kind of chi flow that stimulates your mind into coming up with ideas from deep within you. Once you know this, you can design an atmosphere that will engender the kind of creativity you need. This obviously varies from one person to another, but here are some general ideas that are covered in detail in this section.

• Explore your space until you find the area that has the chi flow you need. An interesting area will be close to windows, as chi moves more strongly here.

• Patterns are mentally stimulating, so fabrics for curtains, cushions and bedding can contribute to your creativity.

• To be able to expand your mental chi, you need space. If you have to be creative at home, you need an area with the broadest horizon, where you can think big thoughts.

• You may find that you need to get out of your home to catalyse certain ideas. Some people find that a museum, cathedral or hotel foyer is the place for this. For others it is climbing a mountain or looking out over the sea.

• There will be times of the day and certain months, in which you should find it easier to conjure up the thoughts you want.

• Loft space is usually a great 'ideas' environment. Being at the top of a building exposes you to more vertical chi.

• You can activate your creative chi internally through meditation and breathing techniques.

• The direction you face while you are seated exposes you to one of the eight directions of chi. By choosing a particular direction, you can absorb more of that chi, making it easier to feel creative.

• Mirrors make a space feel larger and help speed up the flow of chi, resulting in a more lively and stimulating environment.

• The artwork in a room can easily trigger certain thought patterns. You may even build up an association with certain pieces of art and creative feelings.

• Too much clutter stifles the flow of chi – although this is helpful for feeling cosy and settled, it is not ideal when you need that outside stimulus in order to come up with an original idea.

• Sounds transmit chi as they vibrate through the air and into your outer chi field. Certain sounds can stir up your chi in a way that makes you feel more imaginative.

A structured pattern, such as these masks, makes a room feel more yang – ideal for feeling organized.

PLACE YOURSELF IN THE CHI FLOW OF WINDOWS

> **BENEFIT** Refreshes your mental chi

One way in which energy enters and leaves your home is through your windows. By sitting close to a window, you become a part of that flow. Ideally, the front of your body should face the window, so that the incoming chi interacts with the phoenix side of your chi field. The aim is to benefit from the expansive outside chi, making it easier to feel creative. You can adjust the way energy flows into your home by using different types of window treatment.

What you do

1 Experiment with sitting so that you face a window. It is important that the window you choose has an inspiring view. Try to arrange your position so that you also face a helpful direction (see page 216).

2 Keep the windows clean and uncluttered so that chi energy can move freely. Ideally, you will be able to choose between reducing the energy that flows through the windows when you want to settle down and relax and being able to

fully open up the window to allow in as much light as possible when you want to feel more active.

3 Use curtains in situations where you want to calm the flow of chi and create a more cosy, comfortable atmosphere. Wooden blinds make it easier for chi to flow, creating a more dynamic and stimulating atmosphere; and you can angle them to let light through, without receiving the glare of direct sunlight. Fabric

roller blinds have the advantage of leaving the window unobstructed when they are rolled up and providing a softer surface when they are pulled down.

4 You can match the material of your window treatment to the different chi energies present in each part of your home:

• Wooden blinds (north, east, south-east and south).
• Fabric roller blinds or curtains (south, north-east, south-west, west and north-west).

Wooden shutters allow chi to move freely through the window when open.

PATTERNS AND FABRICS

BENEFIT Greater stimulation

Patterns affect the atmosphere of a space and therefore your creativity. In terms of creativity, this is quite personal: bright, loud patterns may increase one person's creativity, whereas a more subtle, mottled effect could be just what another person needs. The main point is to create the effect you desire, and here yin and yang and the five elements help.

These principles can be applied to anything in your home that has a pattern. So wallpaper, curtains, cushions, upholstery and other fabrics can change the chi in a space. This also applies to clothing. If you wear clothing with a pattern on it, the pattern will be inside your own chi field.

What you do

• Remember that large, plain blocks of bright colours are more yang than flowing or intricate patterns. A pattern that is ordered and repeats often is also more yang than something that is irregular.

The floral wall pattern encourages more yin water chi than the yang, wood chi stripes on the table cover.

PATTERNS AND THE ELEMENTS

- **Wood** *Vertical, tall, thin patterns. Helps you feel more uplifted and positive and get greater inspiration from the heavens.*

- **Fire** *Triangular, pointed, serrated patterns. Encourages you to be quick-thinking, with insights into future trends. Good for increasing creativity by bouncing ideas off others.*

- **Soil** *Squat, low, flat horizontal patterns. Makes it easier to focus on the quality of ideas, to think things through carefully and make sure that your creativity is grounded in practicality.*

- **Metal** *Round, domed, arched patterns. Helps you focus on the end result so that your creativity is directed towards something that you can finalize and be rewarded for.*

- **Water** *Irregular, curved, mottled patterns. Helps you access your deepest chi; out of that come original ideas that are personal to you.*

Yang chi can be more stimulating, while yin chi opens up your mind to broader horizons.

- Note that each of the five elements has a pattern associated with it (see above).

- Be aware that the effect of a pattern on the chi of a space will be more powerful when it is used with colour. For example, combining a strong yang pattern and colour (as in a red and yellow diamond pattern) will be dramatic and highly stimulating.

- Don't forget that many patterns are pictorial, such as floral or symbolic patterns – stars in the sky, for instance. Make sure that the imagery you choose has positive associations for you.

OPEN SPACES

BENEFIT Free thinking

Open spaces allow chi to move freely, which make it easier to think clearly. The bigger the space, the greater the freedom the chi will have. This includes the height of ceilings, as well as the floor area. If you live in a small home, you may need to go outside to find those spaces; alternatively, try to create at least one free-thinking area at home in order to improve your creativity. One of the aims when setting up your home is to develop a variety of atmospheres so that you have a space in which to relax, another to get things done in, and somewhere else to feel imaginative.

Well-organized storage can release more space for an open clutter-free environment where chi can expand and flow easily.

What you do

1 Look at your floor plan and use your eight-directions transparency (see pages 112–115) to see if the south-east of your home is a suitable area: this is the ideal part of your home in which to be creative, as its upward chi (associated with the sky and wind) is generally the best for getting those big new ideas. Otherwise, try the south or north. If you have the choice of rooms, use a space with high ceilings and plenty of natural light.

2 Once you have found the best area, clear a space in the centre of the room. Keep only essential furniture there, along with objects that stimulate your imagination.

3 Try to keep surfaces and the floor as empty as possible so that the chi can move freely. Position yourself in this space so that you face a direction that works best for you (see pages 216–217).

4 Ensure that items do not creep back into this space (see page 222 for suggestions on reducing clutter).

GET OUT OF THE HOME TO THINK

BENEFIT Getting a new perspective

Sometimes the best option in order to feel creative is to get out of your home, into a new environment with different chi. Being creative can simply mean getting a new perspective on whatever you are working on, so a change of scene can make all the difference.

You can choose a beneficial direction for you in terms of your year number and find a space that suits your creative needs. Practically speaking, this might be a public space if you need to work on a laptop computer, or outdoors if you just need to refresh your mind and get new ideas.

What you do

1 Look at the section on finding your best directions (see pages 58–61), to establish the ideal direction from your home for the year – and, if you wish, the month as well.

2 Walk in one of your good directions to look for a suitable space. This might be a museum, hotel foyer, café or church. Try to find somewhere with plenty of space so that the chi in your head can open up and reach out for greater creativity. It will help if the interior is inspiring to you. For example, an art gallery might stimulate you, whereas in a café you can refresh your chi with food or drink.

3 If you do not need to be inside, you could look in the countryside for an inspiring place. Trees bring more upward chi and can be useful for greater inspiration. Rivers generate more horizontal chi, which can help you feel inspired by things close to you. A mountain is ideal if you want to get more chi from the cosmos, perhaps leading to that one flash of inspiration and a great idea.

4 When you find your space, remember to use the principles of the five animals (see page 34) to find the best position in which to sit.

When you need to create a special mood you may find that you need to go out to a different building. Here the large space, hard surfaces and minimal furniture all make it easier to expand your chi field so that you can look at bigger issues.

THE BEST TIME TO GET NEW IDEAS

BENEFIT Getting fresh inspiration

At different times of the day, and at different days in the month (or even the coming years), your creativity is different. You therefore have an opportunity to be creative when you feel at your strongest. The key considerations in this respect are the position of the sun and the moon, and mixing your chi with that of the cosmos.

As the sun comes up over the horizon you can experience chi rising and this will help you get fresh new ideas.

What you do

• In terms of the day, try arranging your day so that you can be most creative around sunrise, as this is when chi is rising strongly, activating all your chakras. This chi should result in greater intellectual energy. Try facing east to make the impression on your chi even more powerful.

• Midnight can be helpful in terms of clearing any distractions and being able to relax into a stillness where creative ideas seem to pop into your head from nowhere. Here you could sit facing north to increase the effect.

• At the time of the new moon you should find it easier to reach inside yourself for greater inspiration. This is the ideal time of the month to meditate and use quieter chi to come up with new ideas.

• During the full moon your chi is more active, making it easier to be impulsive and to act on the chi of the moment. You can react to events in real time, and out of that you can interact creatively with your surroundings.

• Using feng shui astrology, you can work out the best months (or even years) when you will have the kind of creativity you need for a certain project. Look at the eight directions for seating (see page 216–217) to identify which direction has the kind of chi you most need. Then go to page 54 to establish which month or year will place you in phase with that particular chi.

LOFT SPACES

BENEFIT Reaching out to the stars for inspiration

The higher up you are in a building, the more you will be exposed to vertical chi from the cosmos. In such spaces you should find it easier to feel inspired and creative than, for example, in a basement. This is because a tall building tends to funnel vertical chi through it, more than a low, squat construction does. In addition, being at the top means that there are fewer obstacles between you and the cosmos.

In a loft space you should feel that you have more ideas spinning around your head, that you can be more original, and that you have a bigger vision in terms of your creativity. Here are some factors to look for in a loft space.

What you do

• A loft space with high ceilings gives the chi more space to move and strengthens the vertical element, so you should find it easier to think freely and reach out for a new perspective.

• Loft spaces with pointed ceilings are more mentally stimulating, as the fiery pyramid shape concentrates and activates the chi inside. This will be even more effective if the ceiling is open and the roof is supported by wooden beams, as the wood feeds the fire-element chi.

• Skylights increase the vertical movement of chi and make it slightly easier to access the chi from the heavens. Ideally the skylights will open, so that you can interact directly with the world above when you need that extra creativity.

• A big, open warehouse-style loft apartment has exceptionally free-flowing chi and, although you may find it harder to feel settled here, you will feel inspired and get many new creative ideas. The challenge is to do something practical with all that creative chi.

In this loft there is a huge amount of free space above your head making it easier to expand your mental chi and broaden your perspective on life.

MEDITATION AND BREATHING

> **BENEFIT** Accesses your deepest creative chi

Sometimes it is when you are completely relaxed and not thinking about anything that you get your best ideas. The principle is that in these moments you are more receptive to the chi outside, and through this you can get the kind of inspiration that you would never imagine you were capable of. This is all about bringing the creativity in from outside, rather than finding it within.

What you do

1 The aim is to breathe in fully. Lie on your back and place your hand over your navel. As you breathe in, expand your abdomen so that you push your hand upwards. Practise this for a while until you can breathe naturally through your abdomen.

2 Fill your abdomen with air and continue to breathe up into your chest. Breathe out all the air from your body on the out-breath.

3 Breathe in quickly and fully within two seconds, hold for one second and then breathe out fully in eight seconds. Repeat several times until you feel energized. You may feel dizzy after a few breaths, so do this sitting or kneeling. Stop as soon as you feel light-headed.

4 Find a comfortable pace and rhythm. Every time you breathe in, imagine that you are drawing in chi from around you – imagine breathing in a colour, a sound or a feeling, and visualize your abdomen and chest turning into that colour, sound or feeling.

5 As you breathe out, imagine your breath filling the space around you. Begin by filling in a small space, and then slowly work up to ultimately filling the whole universe with each breath.

Shutting down your mind and focusing on your connection with the world helps you feel in harmony with your environment.

6 Place a lit candle in front of you and stare into the candle as you meditate. Try to focus all your attention on feeling each breath – the way it feels in your nostrils, mouth, throat and lungs. Once you feel focused, with your mind fully on your breathing, you will absorb chi and ideas into your head.

SITTING DIRECTIONS

BENEFIT Stimulates your creativity

The direction that you face when seated exposes you to one of the eight directions of chi. This will affect your creativity, so it is helpful to know what the particular influence is and whether it is something you need.

What you do

1 Check the direction that you currently face when you are seated, by sitting in your chair, holding your compass with the body pointing away from you and turning the dial so that 0 degrees is lined up with the north end of the needle. Then take a reading from the point where the dial lines up with the centre of the compass body.

2 Note the reading and then look at the eight-directions transparency (see page 113) to establish which direction it relates to. For example, 120 degrees is south-east. You can now look at the relevant direction below to discover its influence.

3 Read through the other directions to see if there is another chi that might help you more.

4 When arranging your seating, remember to protect your back with something like a wall, a big piece of furniture or a large plant, and to keep the area in front of you open.

Directional influences

• **East** Helps to get inspiration and a feeling of creativity rising up through your chakras.

• **South-east** Ideal for major ideas, expanding your horizons and being creative with the biggest issues.

• **South** Cultivates a quick, spontaneous creative mood. Ideal for projecting your creativity.

• **South-west** Best for taking creative ideas and grounding them in reality. Ideal for refining your ideas.

• **West** Good for focusing your creativity and developing a single point to your work.

• **North-west** Helps you feel more intuitive and inspired by the cosmos.

Turn your chair to face the direction with the chi you want whilst maintaining the chi of the animals.

• **North** Excellent for accessing your creativity at its deepest level, and producing individualistic, original work.

• **North-east** Encourages you to pare your ideas down to their purest essence. Ideal for getting rid of peripheral distractions.

MIRRORS

> **BENEFIT** Speeds up and disperses chi

Mirrors and other reflective surfaces change the direction of chi energy in the same way that light is reflected in a new direction. This is helpful when you want to disperse fast-moving chi or reflect more energy into a stagnant area. The aim is to release stale chi, helping you to liberate your creative chi.

There are two types of mirrors that are commonly used: flat mirrors to reflect energy evenly, and round convex mirrors to disperse chi energy in many different directions. The same applies to objects made from polished reflective metal. Reflective concave objects will absorb chi energy into themselves.

What you do

• Hang mirrors in dark spaces where you want to reflect as much of the available light as possible back into the room. This applies to basement spaces, as well as to apartments that only receive northern light.

• Strategically place a mirror so that natural light from a window is reflected back into a dark area of a room or a stagnant corner. You may find this easier with a convex mirror, as it will spread out the light, illuminating the widest possible area of the room.

• Use a mirror to make up for any of the eight directions that appear deficient on your floor plan. Placing your eight-directions transparency over your floor plan (see pages 114–115), see if any of the eight directions are significantly deficient. Place a mirror in the space that is associated with the deficient chi, so that the back of the mirror faces the outside of your home.

• Place a convex mirror or any other convex reflective object in the path of fast-flowing chi to disperse the energy into areas of your home where the chi is thinner.

A convex mirror sends chi out in a wide arc, helping to disperse chi throughout the room.

ARTWORK

BENEFIT Stimulates the mind

Use works of art to stimulate your mind and draw out your creativity. Blocks of bright colours, abstract images and simplistic imagery are often associated with creativity, although an impressionist painting, a classic sculpture or a household object can be equally stimulating. The aim is to surround yourself with items that trigger off creative feelings whenever you see them.

What you do

• Every time you buy something for your home, make sure that you find the design interesting and that it contributes to your creative instincts. You could apply this to objects such as lamp stands, coffee tables and candle holders.

• Try to visit art galleries, antique shops and junk stores to find that special object that gets your creative juices flowing. Sometimes filling your home with bland artwork can dissipate your creativity and dilute the effect of anything that does resonate with creative chi, so it is better to be selective and go for a few quality items.

• Apply your creative eye to everything possible in your home. This might include fabrics for cushions, curtains and bedding, door handles and even the radiators.

• Aim to fill your home with individualistic one-off art items, rather than mass-produced objects. Your home will probably already have a wealth of mass-produced equipment, such as televisions, music systems and kitchen equipment, so it will be inspiring to make your home unique to you through its artwork.

• See if you can use your creativity to think of that one thing that will help define your home as a creative space. You might have a clock projected onto a wall, a floor constructed from a mixture of materials, or big colourful prints hanging on your walls. Whatever it is, try to make it yours so that each time you come home you get that creative feeling.

This painting has upward wood movement with a dynamic yang feel. Just looking at it could help you feel uplifted.

DE-CLUTTER

BENEFIT More room in which to think

One of the aims of enhancing your creativity is to encourage chi to move harmoniously through your home and avoid situations where it stagnates, as stagnant chi is the antithesis of creativity.

One of the things that makes chi stagnate is clutter. Too much clutter restricts the movement of chi so that it loses momentum. Clutter hangs on to chi, and keeps it in the same place for a long time, leading to a stuffy feeling in a room, where it is harder to move forward and try new things. A person living in a very cluttered home can feel that everything is a struggle and they are stuck in a rut, losing their creativity completely.

What you do

1 Have a major springclean – take everything out of its place and clean all those dark corners, stirring up the chi that has lain dormant there.

2 Get a number of large cardboard boxes and label each one with today's date. Write on them 'long-term storage', 'letting go' and 'undecided'.

3 Put all the things that you think you will not need for some time in the 'long-term storage' box. These will be items that you cannot throw away, but which you are unlikely to need access to (such as old bank statements).

4 Take the box marked 'letting go' and put in it all the items that remind you of a part of your history that you wish to leave behind.

5 Take the 'undecided' box and put into it all the objects that clutter your home, but which you think you might miss.

6 After a month throw out those things you have not missed from the 'letting go' box. Keep the other two boxes for another month, then look through them to see if you can transfer anything from 'undecided' to 'long-term storage'. See if you feel comfortable parting with the contents of the 'undecided' box.

Getting rid of dust removes the chi attached to it, allowing space for fresh chi to come into your home.

FILL THE ATMOSPHERE WITH SOUND WAVES

> **BENEFIT** Greater inspiration and creativity

Any sound waves vibrating through the air will also pass through your own outer chi field. The frequency of the sound waves will influence your chi, helping to change your mood and potentially your creativity. A softer, more gentle, yin sound will soothe and calm the chi around you, making it easier to focus more deeply inside for that creative solution. More vibrant, rhythmic, yang sounds will activate your outer chi field, making it easier to bring your creativity up to the surface and express it.

What you do

• Think carefully when you play music (one of the most common sounds at home), as this is an opportunity to help stimulate your emotions. There may be certain pieces of music that you know help you feel inspired and creative. Sometimes this could be due to association – the music reminds you of a time when you were particularly creative – or it could simply be that the sound waves resonate with your chi in a way that makes you feel more imaginative.

• Before you add anything to your home that makes a sound (for instance, a telephone, alarm clock or doorbell), ensure that it has a tone you like. From a feng shui perspective, such sounds are better if they use a traditional metal bell, as this helps clear and stimulate the atmosphere each time it rings.

• Consider bringing in other ambient sounds that you like. This might be the sound of an indoor waterfall or the rhythmic ticking of a clock. Such sounds will ripple out through your home, keeping the chi on the move and thereby reducing the risk of stagnation.

The sound of running water will fill your home with a relaxing multi-frequency sound that subdues other noises.

FENG SHUI AND
YOUR FINANCES

HOW YOUR HOME CAN HELP YOU BE FINANCIALLY AWARE

Feng shui is helpful in terms of setting the scene so that you can improve your finances. However, to make this succeed, you need to work on yourself to be a more financially aware person – it is unlikely that feng shui will simply make money come to you out of the blue.

Think through ways in which you can increase your wealth. Do you need to earn more, save more or spend less? If you need to earn more, consider

how you can make this happen. If you are in regular employment, do you need a new venture, to get a promotion or ask for a rise? How do you see yourself increasing your long-term wealth? Are you working on an opportunity that could bring in a large one-off payment? Or is it a slow build-up or a question of maintaining what you have?

Once you have a clear idea of how you can become wealthier, look at ways in which you can work on yourself to increase your opportunities. If you have already tried but failed, you will have more experience to go on; if you are just starting, you will need to use your imagination more.

Make a list of characteristics that you could change about yourself to make it easier to be wealthy. For example, do you need to be more assertive, work harder, have a more ruthless streak, concentrate more on profits, be better at completing projects, be more disciplined about saving money, or value yourself more? In this section you will learn how to bring greater focus to your finances.

• Use coins to stimulate the chi associated with bringing money in.

• Increase the chi associated with wealth by using money plants.

• Get every part of your home to work for you.

• Stop the chi of wealth slipping out through your front door.

• Create a situation where you have more opportunities to improve your finances.

• Boost the chi you need in order to start new ventures.

• Strengthen the chi that helps you increase your income.

• Use feng shui to help you save more of your income.

• Activate the chi that increases the flow of money.

Keep a focus on what you want money for so that the money you earn has real value to you.

COINS ON A RED CLOTH

BENEFIT Increases the focus on your finances

The chi of the west is associated with the sunset and harvest time. This is when you get the rewards for work done during the day or year, so this chi is ideal for bringing things to a profitable conclusion. One of the ways to increase your ability to focus and put energy into improving your finances is to boost the chi in the west part of your home.

You can do this by placing some coins or bank notes on a red cloth in the west. The metal that the coins are made of, along with the colour red, will add more metal energy to this metal-chi direction. The coins and bank notes will also serve as a symbolic reminder of this particular aspect of your life.

Use your favourite coins, the larger the denomination the greater your ambition. Use coins from other countries if you want to travel.

What you do

1 Look at your floor plan and correctly align your eight-directions transparency over the centre (see pages 114–115), so that you can see where the west segment of your home lies. If this is not suitable for the coins, because it is a bathroom, utility room or store, choose the north-western or northern segment.

2 Find a prominent place within the room and lay out a red cloth. Place the highest bank note in whatever currency you are using on the cloth, then put the highest-denomination coins on top.

3 If you do not want to use bank notes, you can simply put the coins in a metal bowl on the red cloth. To keep the chi of the coins moving, take out some of the coins and refill with new ones weekly.

4 Alternatively, you can use Chinese coins. These have a square hole in the centre, so you can tie a red ribbon through several coins and hang them in the west part of your home. They need to have a similar symbolism to coins from your own currency in order to be as effective.

MONEY PLANTS

BENEFIT Increases the chi associated with making money

Each part of your home has a different influence on your ability to increase your wealth. For example, the east helps you come up with new ways to earn money; the south-east looks at ways to increase your prosperity in the future; and the north-east enables you to seize the opportunity to make a profitable investment.

One way to activate the chi in each area is to use a money plant. Its rounded leaves are associated with metal chi, which in turn is linked to coins and money. To make the effect stronger, you can grow the plant in a metal container, or support the metal chi by potting the plant in a clay pot, representing soil chi.

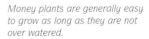

Money plants are generally easy to grow as long as they are not over watered.

What you do

1 Align your eight-directions transparency over the centre of your floor plan to find where the eight directions in your home are (see pages 114–115).

2 Place your money plant in your chosen area to activate the chi. The following list of the eight directions gives you ideas on how a particular direction can help financially, and what to do in that part of your home.

Directional qualities

• **East** Helps you start new money-making projects and expand your business.

• **South-east** Increases your ability to acquire new ideas concerning your future prosperity.

• **South** Helps develop the passion to go out and earn money. Good for developing useful contacts.

• **South-west** Use this area to focus on your savings and find ways to make the money you have go further.

• **West** Makes it easier to make more money out of what you are already doing to earn money.

• **North-west** Good for acquiring more integrity about money and greater respect for its value.

• **North** Increases the chi that relates to your cashflow. Ideal if people are slow in paying you.

• **North-east** This is the winner's chi and is great for quick decisions. Increase this chi if you want to speculate.

GET YOUR WHOLE HOME TO WORK FOR YOU

BENEFIT Improves every aspect of your finances

As we have seen (see pages 232–233), each part of your home has an influence on your ability to increase your wealth. The following list further explains the significance of each direction and gives you ideas on what objects to use in each part of your home.

More on directional attributes

• **East** Place a moving water feature there to help you start new money-making projects. Put a shiny coin in the water at the beginning of the day when you feel close to a breakthrough.

• **South-east** Put a bowl of fresh water on top of the largest bank note in your currency to get new ideas for your future prosperity. Refill the bowl as soon as you get up each day.

• **South** Hang pictures of things that motivate you to earn more money. These images should be inspirational and should keep you focused on the future.

• **South-west** Use a clay pot to keep your savings-account details in, or simply keep a yellow flowering plant in a clay container to boost this direction's energy.

• **West** Put shiny coins on a red cloth to increase this chi, making it easier to make money. This also helps you have fun and enjoy making money.

• **North-west** Keep your financial information in this part of your home, if you want to get serious about your finances. This area is good for understanding the value of money.

• **North** Hang a small, round multi-faceted crystal in this part of your home to increase the chi that relates to your cashflow.

• **North-east** This is the chi for quick decisions. If you like to speculate and play the stock market, increase this chi by keeping your share certificates here, along with a large rock (white crystal is best).

Keep things that inspire you in the south so that they pick up the fiery chi there. By facing south as you look at them you will pick up more fire chi.

STAIRS AND DOORS

BENEFIT Conserves your money

Chi breathes between the floors of your home, and most of this chi flows between the floors via the stairs. As people walk up and down the stairs, they stir up the chi, creating a natural path for it to flow along. The stairs are usually a channel of fast-moving chi and determine how some of the energy enters and leaves each floor.

Broad open stairs encourage the chi energy to move faster. Stone and polished hardwood stairs encourage energy to move quickly across the surface; bare wooden stairs have a more neutral influence; and carpets, seagrass and rush matting slow the flow of chi.

As chi picks up speed moving along the stairs, it is important to consider what this fast-moving chi will meet as it leaves. If it is directed towards your front door when it reaches the bottom of the stairs, it tends to rush out of your home, with the result that your home becomes deficient in chi. This can make it harder to retain your money, so that it seems difficult to build up your savings. The remedy is to redirect some of the chi from your front door and spread it into other areas of your home.

What you do

• If your stairs lead to your front door, walk downstairs slowly looking for a suitable location for a small, round convex mirror (it can be about the size of the palm of your hand). Hang the mirror so that it faces you as you descend the stairs.

• Grow a bushy plant between the foot of your stairs and the door to slow down the passage of chi.

• Hang a wind chime so that it rings when the front door is opened. This will spread the chi throughout your home, reducing the risk of it flowing out of your door.

Open stairs, like these, allow chi to spread out as it flows between the floors, whereas enclosed stairs channel chi in a more focused direction.

REAP MORE FINANCIAL OPPORTUNITIES

BENEFIT Strengthens your financial chi

The quick, reactive chi of the north-east is ideal for spotting new investment opportunities. This energy also helps you seize the moment before others can react. The chi of the north-east is sharp and piercing, like a bitter wind, helping you to cut straight to the point. At the same time you need to be more yang in order to remain focused, precise and alert, which will in turn help you react quickly.

What you do

• To expose yourself to more north-eastern chi, sleep with the top of your head pointing north-east. However, this will not work if you are a light sleeper or suffer from nightmares – in which case, try pointing west for greater financial awareness. Placing yourself at work so that you face north-east will also help.

• Putting decorative stones or rocks close to you will generate more north-eastern energy, which is associated with the mountain. A brilliant white colour further stimulates this chi. Try painting walls and ceiling white, using more white flowers, or putting white crystal rocks in the north-east segment of your home.

• Fire chi nourishes the north-eastern chi and is helpful in enabling you to spot future trends. To increase this chi, use a bright fiery purple and bright lights. Plants with pointed leaves will further increase this energy.

• Create a more yang atmosphere where the chi moves faster by creating large open spaces, using bright colours and hard surfaces, so that you feel alert and active.

• You may find that your best year or month for spotting opportunities is when your year number is to the north-east. Check on page 53 to see when this next occurs.

Rocks and stones in the north-east will strengthen the quick soil chi there, helping you be more quick minded.

START NEW VENTURES

> **BENEFIT** Brings greater energy to begin fresh projects

To successfully start a new career you need enthusiasm, confidence and the belief that you can make it happen. These qualities are found in the chi of the east. To help you get off to the best start, you need to bring more eastern energy into your own chi field. This sunrise, springtime, upward-moving chi makes it easier to feel like taking on new money-making projects.

A glass bowl is ideal for your fresh water as the glass is also associated with water chi.

What you do

• Place a bowl of water in the east part of your home. Refill it each morning so that you bring in more fresh-water energy. Water is supportive of the wood chi of the east and increases the presence of this morning, springtime energy. This will be even more powerful if you can position the bowl so that the morning sun hits it.

• You can also increase eastern chi by growing plants in the east – the plants represent wood energy and bring in more of that chi.

• Another effective way to absorb eastern chi is to work facing east so that you can directly bring this energy into your own chi energy field. If this is not possible, try facing south-east.

• Whenever you want to start something new, it is essential to clear the decks for action – this means getting rid of everything you no longer need and making the space for something new to happen. Once you have the extra space, it is easier to feel that you have the capacity to take on a new venture. It is much harder to start something when you are cramped for space and still surrounded by the clutter from your previous projects.

Facing east helps you absorb a powerful chi for starting new projects.

INCREASE YOUR INCOME

BENEFIT Enhances your money-making potential

The west part of your home is associated with the desire to be wealthy, feeling romantic and being content, while the north-west relates to feeling in control, being organized and acting with wisdom. These aspects of your life could be disrupted if you have anything that generates fire chi there. This might be a boiler, cooker (gas or electric), fireplace or an oven.

The west and north-west areas are associated with metal chi, and its energy can be destroyed by fire chi when there is a deficiency of soil chi. The solution is to add more soil chi to harmonize the fire and metal chi. The easiest way to do this is by using something that generates strong soil chi energy. A convenient option is to put some charcoal in a clay pot (I suggest taking a stick of artist's charcoal and breaking it into chunks). This can be further enhanced by placing the pot on a yellow cloth.

Other items that will help are anything made of clay, or an object that is yellow and has a low, flat shape. In addition, earth for plants carries soil energy. A yellow flowering plant in a clay container harnesses all these attributes.

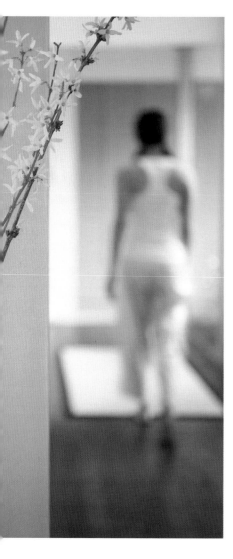

What you do

1 Use your floor plan and eight-directions transparency to find the west and north-west segments of your home (see pages 114–115). Look in these directions to see if you have anything that generates fire chi.

2 If you have located such objects, place your clay pot with charcoal in it on a yellow cloth as close as possible to the boiler, cooker, fireplace or oven. In the case of a cooker or fireplace, position the charcoal on either side. With a boiler, place the charcoal on a shelf or on the floor below. For an oven, place the charcoal in a cupboard as close by as possible.

3 Change the charcoal approximately every two months and keep the area around the clay pot clean and clear.

Yellow flowers are associated with soil chi. When placed in the west they support the metal chi there, helping you focus on increasing your wealth.

SAVE MORE

BENEFIT Increases your ability to save

It is important to ensure that the atmosphere of your home encourages you to be aware of your finances and how to use your money effectively. The south-western chi associated with this is represented by the sun descending in the afternoon. In feng shui this relates to the energy of the autumn, when animals are saving their food for the winter, making it ideal for this gathering and storing-type activity. This chi is more abundant in the south-west part of your home.

What you do

• To help activate the south-western chi, place yellow flowers or a yellow flowering plant in south-west part of your home. This will be even more effective if you use a clay container to keep them in.

• Use yellow, brown or black fabrics for cushions, curtains or tablecloths in the south-west part of your home. This promotes a feeling of being settled and comfortable with putting money to one side for the future.

• Try sleeping with the top of your head pointing south-west for a while to absorb more of this stable chi. In addition, try sitting facing this direction.

• You can lose chi by letting energy flow out of your home too easily. Leaking taps increase this risk, particularly if they are in the south-west part of your home. So fix any leaks promptly.

• When you do spend money, try to buy things that will hold their value or increase their value over the years. Antiques, paintings, classic cars, houses and jewellery all have the potential to do this.

• It will be easiest to save money in a year or month when your year number is in the south-west (see page 53).

Yellow will strengthen the chi in the south-west making it easier to save and conserve your wealth.

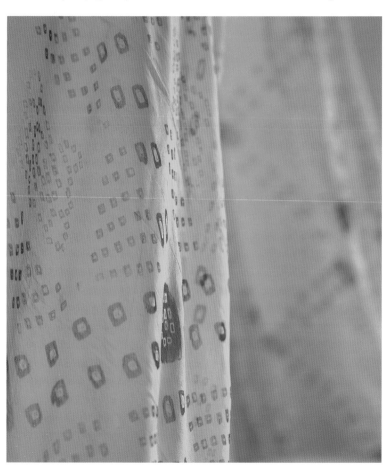

LET THE MONEY FLOW

BENEFIT Being a part of the financial flow

Money flows around the globe with a chi of its own. It has become a powerful means of connection across the planet as it passes from one person to another. You only have to look at the origin of many of the goods you buy to realize how the money you have paid will spread across various countries.

If you want to be a part of this flow of chi around the world, you need to position yourself so that you can earn and spend money – this is best identified as water chi. The flow of money mirrors the flow of water around the planet. Once you are part of the flow, you have the opportunity to influence the direction in which humans are heading, every time you spend your money (for example, by buying organic foods rather than those treated with chemicals).

What you do

• To absorb more northern water chi into your energy field, sleep with the top of your head pointing north, or sit facing this direction.

• Place a moving water feature in the north, east or south-east segment of your home. Use your floor plan and transparency to find these directions (see pages 112–115). The moving water will increase the flow of chi, making you better able to pick up on money flowing around you.

• You will be in the ideal position to feel part of the flow of money in a year or month when your year number is in the north.

• Hang a crystal in a window in the north part of your home to stimulate the northern chi here. Try to position it so that it catches some morning or evening sunlight.

*A large mirror in the north of the
room helps stimulate chi there.*

FENG SHUI AND MOVING HOME

CHOOSE THE RIGHT HOME FOR YOU

Moving home is one of the biggest potential life-changing events. You immerse yourself in a completely different chi and inevitably find that your life alters as a result. The greater the distance you move, the greater the potential for change. Moving to a different culture makes for an even bigger dramatic shift in your life. If you are buying your new home, it probably represents the largest investment you will ever make.

For these reasons it is essential to get the move right, in a direction that is favourable for you at that time, and into a home that has the kind of chi in which you can flourish. Here are some of the prime considerations that are covered in greater detail in this section.

• Find out what happened to the people who lived there before. Ideally they will have had a good relationship, happy children and financial success. Some homes have a history of families splitting up, or a run of people who have had financial troubles. These homes should be avoided unless you can see why this happened from a feng shui perspective and know how to remedy it.

• Avoid moving into a home that is near electrical pylons or an electrical sub-station, because there is little you can do to overcome the potentially harmful electromagnetic fields. Similarly, living next to electric railway tracks, a nuclear processing plant or anywhere exposed to toxic waste will be hazardous.

• Look at the properties of the various directions (see page 36) and decide which directions would help you most. See if you can find a home that faces one of these directions, as more of this chi will then enter your house or apartment.

• Try and get a well-proportioned home with an almost square floor plan. This will make it easier to live a well-balanced life.

• Get a home with good exposure to natural light and sunlight. In a city this often means being higher up in a building, so that you are not in the shadow of other buildings. In rural areas, choose a home that has space around it.

• Make sure your prospective home contains as many natural materials as possible, especially if it is a new one, because many synthetic materials give off toxic fumes for years, filling your new home with unhealthy gases.

Moving home can be one of those life-changing events, so it is important to try to make sure they are the changes you want.

PLANT YOURSELF IN A NEW ENVIRONMENTAL CHI

> **BENEFIT** Positive life changes

When you have lived for some time in a home, you will have absorbed the chi of that space and will have projected some of your own chi back into it. For this reason your chi will be similar to the chi of your house. Your home will have a part of your emotional energy within it, and a part of your home will have defined your chi. When you move, you pull yourself out of this familiar chi and put yourself into a new chi. If you move to a home that has been inhabited by someone else, you also immerse yourself in the chi he or she has left behind. This makes a house move an incredible opportunity to change your chi and move your life forward. But there is a risk that if this does not result in you taking in a better chi, you may find your life going in an undesirable direction.

One of the easiest ways to get a feel for the chi of a potential new home is to do a little research on its residents.

What you do

• Try to meet the current residents, so that you get a feel for the kind of chi they have projected into the home. See if you get an impression of their physical health, mental well-being and emotional happiness just by meeting them. If they are a couple, you may be able to gain an impression of how they relate to each other.

• You can also search local records or the Internet to see if there is more information that you should be aware of.

• If you cannot meet the current residents, talk to neighbours to get a feel for what they are (or were) like. It would be helpful to find out about any health issues, marital problems or financial challenges.

A home with happy, healthy people living there will inevitably have that kind of chi.

CHOOSE YOUR LOCATION

> **BENEFIT** Finding the chi that helps you most

Over time, civilizations have built up in areas of different chi and have therefore developed reputations for excellence in a certain field, because the particular chi there has made it easier to excel at something – perhaps art, banking, writing or trading.

It may be that certain types of chi flow are better suited to certain professions. For example, strong vertical chi might suit writers, who work on their own and need inspiration, originality and imagination. Conversely, a trader might be better supported by a horizontal chi flow, as he or she tries to interact strongly with other people.

If you know what you want to do in life and are planning to move, you can focus on places that are most likely to help you.

This dramatic sky line shows the tall wood chi tower, the metal chi dome, the soil chi low flat-roofed homes, the fire chi spire and water chi irregular shapes.

What you do

1 Do some initial research on the Internet to find locations where people whom you wish to emulate have lived. Then see if any of these locations coincide with places where you wish to live. As everything goes through cycles, it is best to focus your enquiries on living people.

2 Once you have a choice of locations, look up their histories. You can often find books or pamphlets that give a description of the different kinds of activities that have thrived there over the centuries. You should also be able to determine whether this is in an ascendant or declining phase.

3 Visit the area to determine whether it has the kind of atmosphere you feel would be supportive to you. Spend time out in the open; try different cafés and public buildings to soak up the local chi.

4 Meet some local people – ideally in the profession of your choice – and see if they seem to thrive in this location.

HILLS AND WATER

BENEFIT Support from the forces of nature

Both hills and water have a dramatic influence on the local chi. Hills encourage a greater vertical component in the chi flow, and large rivers a stronger horizontal flow (the exception is a waterfall, which encourages chi to move downwards).

It therefore makes sense to thoroughly investigate these issues when looking for a new home. You can often get all this information from a detailed map, which will show you the heights of the areas you are interested in, along with any bodies of water.

What you do

1 When choosing to live in a hilly or mountainous area, it is best to choose a home that has the hill behind you and faces an open vista, so that you have the protection of the chi represented by the tortoise behind you and the open chi of the phoenix in front of you (see page 34).

2 Look on a map to establish if any water runs close to your home. You could also ask the local authorities for information on any underground waterways.

3 In the case of surface water, visit the area and check that it is clean and unpolluted. The water is more likely to be healthy if it moves freely and has fish and other aquatic life in it.

4 Check in what direction the water lies from the centre of your home, and estimate how close it is. If the surface water is very close to your home – say, within 50 m (165 ft) – it will be better if it is to the east or south-east of your home.

5 If your enquiries reveal that underground water runs directly below your home and relatively close to the surface – within 2 m (6½ ft) – find out if the water carries sewage or clean water.

A hilly terrain makes it easier to be independent and individualistic. Use the concept of the five animals for ideas on the facing direction.

RAILWAYS AND ROADS

> **BENEFIT** Avoiding disturbed chi

Trains and cars moving along the surface stir up the natural flow of chi. This can be helpful in terms of feeling connected to society at large, but perhaps the greater risk is that you will find it harder to relax and feel settled if your home is close to this spinning chi.

The busier the road or railway line, the greater the influence on your home (quiet roads or railways will not have much effect). Another consideration with railways is whether or not they are powered by electricity. If so, the electricity will generate electromagnetic fields, which could compromise your health (see pages 142–143). And vehicles will produce unhealthy fumes, which also make it harder to maintain good health.

What you do

1 Check on your map for any indications of a railway line. If there is a line close by (closer than 1 km/½ mile), inspect the tracks and see if it is powered by electricity. If this is the case, the tracks need to be at least 800 m (870 yd) away; if not, then a quiet track should be about 500 m (550 yd) away.

2 Check the roads nearby. Any busy main roads should be at least 500 m (550 yd) away, and motorways even further to ensure that the chi near your home is not chaotic and that you are not exposed to unhealthy fumes.

3 See if any roads lead straight to your home, so that vehicles drive directly towards it. This will stir up chi and direct it into your home, making the chi there much more intense. Again, this will only be a consideration if the road is busy and has fast-moving chi.

Living on a curved road means that vehicles will drive straight towards your home, directing chi at you. This can make it harder to relax and feel settled.

ELECTRICITY AND CHI POLLUTERS

BENEFIT Avoiding polluted chi

Two potentially harmful substances that are difficult to remedy are electromagnetic fields and toxic waste. Both can have a negative influence on your health, and children will be most at risk. It is therefore important to determine whether these are an issue with any potential new home at the outset, because they are the two things that can make a living space undesirable from a feng shui perspective.

Another concern would be a nuclear electrical power plant or reprocessing plant. Should there be any leakage, the closer you are, the greater the risk of harmful exposure to nuclear radiation.

What you do

1 Research with your local electricity provider and local authorities to establish whether there are any high-voltage cables or transformers close to your potential home.

2 Arrange for the electromagnetic fields in and around your home to be measured so that you can assess the risk. Compare the data from the measurements with those provided on authoritative websites. Your electricity provider may be able to conduct the inspection for you.

3 Check local-authority records for any evidence of toxic spillage in the area. If you are buying a home built in the last 50 years, check to discover what the site was used for previously and whether it could have been contaminated by toxic waste.

4 Research the wider area to find out if there are any nuclear reactors, reprocessing plants or storage facilities within a 20-km (15-mile) radius. Anything within this distance makes a home there potentially risky. Again, children will be most at risk.

5 Check for industries that could pollute the area either through the air or water. Chemical plants are a risk in terms of air-borne pollution, fires and explosion. Similarly, living close to power stations that emit high levels of carbon dioxide is best avoided.

Be careful of moving to a home that is subjected to EMF as there is little you can do to improve the situation with feng shui.

LOOK AT YOUR HOME FROM THE OUTSIDE

> **BENEFIT** Getting to know the chi of your home

The outside of your home provides many clues to the fundamental chi inside. The primary considerations are how the shape of a house influences the chi inside, and in what way the windows predicate the chi flow in and out of the house.

What you do

1 Look at the house or, if you are buying an apartment, the building, from the outside to see its shape in profile (see opposite). Most buildings have a mixture of different types of chi. For example, a low home with a pointed roof has soil and fire chi.

2 If you notice that there are two opposite elements in a building (such as a tall building with a domed roof), you need to think of ways to bring in the harmonizing chi (in this example, wood and metal are harmonized by water). It is unusual for this ever to happen.

3 Observe the number and size of the windows. The more windows there are, and the bigger they are, the easier it is for chi to flow in and out of the home. This reduces the risk of stagnation, but can make it harder to feel settled there. Windows encourage a more horizontal flow of chi.

This building has the potential for strong horizontal chi with the large windows, flat roof and horizontal features.

Chi and house shapes

• If it is tall with high ceilings, there will be plenty of upward, vertical chi, creating more wood chi inside.

• A pointed roof indicates there will be more fire chi inside. The steeper the roof, the stronger the effect.

• If the roof is low and wide, there will be more settled, horizontal chi, representing soil chi.

• A domed roof, round windows or arches suggest there will be more metal chi, containing the atmosphere inside.

• An irregular shape, where there have been many different additions to the house over the years, is associated with water chi.

SURVEY THE SITE

BENEFIT More harmonious chi

There are three considerations with regard to other buildings close to your home.

1 Do they rob your home of any natural sunlight? This occurs if they are taller than your home and are positioned to the east, south-east, south, south-west or west. This can cause a deficiency of chi in your home and deny you some of the chi of that particular direction.

2 Does the corner of any building point towards your house, directing fast-flowing chi at your home? This will make it harder to feel settled and comfortable at home.

3 Is your home close to another with an opposing element? (See pages 262–263 for details of which type of home has a profile associated with which of the five elements.) There is a risk of disharmony if the missing elements are not represented.

What you do

1 If your home is in the shadow of another building, check the direction of the sunlight that is being blocked. Look on page 36 to see what kind of chi you will have a deficiency of, and whether this is something that is important to you.

2 Assess whether you can plant trees, bushes or a hedge between your home and the corner of the other building, to damp down the chi spinning towards your home.

3 Look at the shape of your building – most homes have soil with a fire-shaped roof – and see if there are other shapes that could be in conflict. For instance, an irregular water-shaped building would not be harmonious next to a fire, soil-shaped home unless there was wood chi present in the form of plants and trees.

The glass surface of this office will speed up chi and potentially make the surrounding atmosphere less comfortable.

THE FACING DIRECTION

> **BENEFIT** Knowing the chi that flows in

The direction that your house or apartment faces determines which kind of chi predominantly flows into your home. In some situations this will be the most dominant force; in others it will be a relatively minor consideration. Those homes where the chi obviously comes in from one direction will be most strongly influenced by which type of chi it is.

A home that has several different directions of chi coming in will have a better balance and will therefore be less influenced by any single direction of chi. For example, a square home with windows and doors on all sides will be relatively balanced, whereas a wide home with little depth, large windows and a door on one side will be highly influenced by the chi of its facing direction.

What you do

1 Walk around the home to see if the four façades are of similar size and whether the doors and windows are evenly spread out. Is there plenty of space around the home, so that chi can enter evenly? If this is the case, the facing direction will not be a primary consideration.

2 If you feel the chi is predominantly entering from one direction (because, for example, the entrance to the site, the drive, the main entrance and front façade with large windows all encourage a strong flow of chi from one direction), you need to take a compass reading to determine which chi it is. Stand with your back to the facing direction and point the body of your compass directly away from

you. Turn the dial so that 0 degrees lines up with the north point of the needle. Take the reading from the point where the dial lines up with the compass body. Look at your eight-directions transparency (see pages 112–115) and on page 36 to see what kind of chi will enter your home.

The front door, path, road and windows clearly make this the front of this home and this would be where most chi enters.

MOVING DIRECTIONS

> **BENEFIT** Moving into a more helpful chi

Finding the time to move in a particular direction, or directions, will charge up your chi in a way that helps you feel better able to fulfil your life's dreams. The further you move, the more important this becomes. A move of less than 1 km (½ mile) will have little noticeable effect, regardless of the direction. A move across continents to a different culture will have the greatest influence, resulting in a potentially life-changing event. You will find a more detailed description of how to work through the process of moving on page 58.

What you do

1 To check when to move in a particular direction, find a map that has both your home and your proposed destination on it. Mark both with an X.

2 Place the centre of your eight-directions transparency (see pages 112–115) on the X that marks your home, then turn the transparency so that north is pointing towards the top of the page. See in which sector the X that marks your destination lies.

3 Look on page 58 to work out in which years and months that direction becomes favourable to you.

4 Alternatively, to determine which directions are favourable to you in a particular year, take a map and mark your home with an X.

5 Place the centre of your transparency on the X that marks your home, then turn the transparency so that north is pointing towards the top of the page.

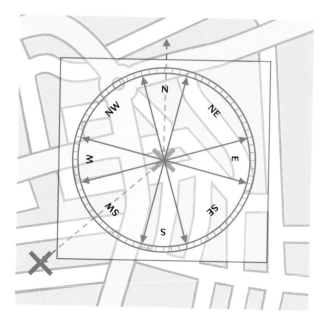

6 Work through the process on page 58 to find out which directions are suitable for you during the year in which you are interested.

7 Look at the appropriate directions on your map to locate possible areas to move to.

Your eight direction transparency is a quick way to check the directions from your home on any map.

GOOD FENG SHUI CHECKLIST

BENEFIT Getting the right home

Photocopy this checklist so that you can take it with you when you view a potential new home.

What you do

☐ **1** Check that the potential new home is in a beneficial direction for you.

☐ **2** Look at a map to see if there are any rivers, lakes, reservoirs, railway lines, industrial plants or nuclear installations nearby.

☐ **3** Check out the local area for power lines, electrical installations, main roads, ponds and streams close to the home.

☐ **4** Find out as much as you can about the current occupants.

☐ **5** Look from the outside to see what kind of chi the home might have inside.

☐ **6** Think about the profile of the home in terms of the five elements, and see if there are any potential conflicts with other homes next door.

☐ 7 Check whether any other buildings have a corner pointing towards the home in which you are interested.

☐ 8 Look at the outside of the premises to determine whether most of the chi comes from a certain direction. If that is the case, take a compass reading to see which chi is predominant.

☐ 9 As you enter the home, look to see if the stairs come directly towards you, directing chi out of the front door.

☐ 10 As you walk around the home, try to absorb the chi and get a sense of how you feel there.

☐ 11 Examine the way light comes into the home, and see if anything blocks sunlight from the house. If this is the case, use your compass to find out which chi might be deficient.

☐ 12 Try to get a sense of the floor plan (or look at an existing one, if available), so that you can determine whether there is an even mix of chi or whether some energies are deficient.

☐ 13 Size up how much work will be required to bring a natural feel to the space.

☐ 14 Estimate the position of all the water and fire elements so that you can consider whether remedies will be required.

RITUALS WHEN YOU MOVE IN

> **BENEFIT** Clears out old chi

When you move to a new home, it can help you get a fresh start if you clear out all the old chi left by the previous occupants. The ideal time to do this is while your new home is still empty, before all the furniture arrives.

What you do

1 While you do your packing, try to get rid of any unwanted clutter, so that when you arrive you just bring the things you really need into your new home.

2 The quickest and most dramatic way to clear out old chi is to give your new home a complete springclean. This will be much easier if the space is empty. Try to get every bit of the old dirt and dust out of each room. It is best to do this on a dry, sunny day so that the sun can naturally refresh the atmosphere. Keep the windows open to encourage fresh chi to blow through your home.

3 If you are keeping any of the carpets, give them a shampoo as this is where most of the dust and stagnant energy tends to collect. It is even worth washing the walls, if you feel up to it.

4 Hand bells are useful for stirring up old, stagnant chi. Take a hand bell and ring it in all the corners and anywhere that dust usually collects. The sound waves will help get the chi moving again and will encourage fresh chi into those areas. Alternatively, you can clap your hands smartly while letting out a powerful fast breath to get chi moving more quickly.

5 Soak up the old chi of your new home using sea salt. Sprinkle sea salt on the floor before you go to bed. In the morning vacuum or sweep up the salt and take it out of the home straight away to get rid of the negative chi energy. You can repeat this exercise several times, until you feel that your new space has a fresh, clean atmosphere.

The more ways you can find to get old chi out of your new home the easier it will be to fill it with your own chi.

MAKE YOUR NEW HOME YOURS

BENEFIT Blends your home with your personality

Your mental and emotional chi not only fills your head, but expands out into the space around you. This makes it possible to fill your home with your chi so that your house becomes an extension of your mental and emotional self. To change the atmosphere with your own chi you need to radiate positive thoughts out into your new home.

What you do

1 Meditate and focus your mind strongly on what you are trying to achieve in life. Each time you breathe out, imagine that you are breathing those thoughts out into the room and that your ideas are coating every surface, painting the walls.

2 Light a candle and focus your meditation on the candle. This will help spread your chi out more easily, because your thoughts become attached to the light waves radiating out into the room. To do this, sit or kneel in front of a lit candle and focus into the flame all the positive things you want to achieve in this space.

Each time you breathe out, try to channel your chi into the root of the flame.

3 The sound of a bell will help send your own chi energy out further. As you ring the bell, the sound waves ripple through your thinking space, carrying your chi energy with them. So keep a hand bell with you and ring it when you have a thought or feeling that you want to send out strongly.

4 Similarly, chanting will throw out more strongly your chi and your emotions. Try making aaah, oooh and mmm sounds as you meditate.

Here the purple colours and candle produce strong fire chi which helps you get your emotional chi out into the environment.

FENG SHUI AND YOUR FAMILY

CREATE THE IDEAL ATMOSPHERE FOR YOUR FAMILY

The home you grow up in tends to be a major influence on your formative years. Homes contain family life, but are also defined by it. There is a huge difference between visiting the homes of people who have children and of those who do not. Family homes live and breathe life. If you have a family, it is important to try and create the best atmosphere for your children, because the rest of their lives will be coloured by their experiences there.

In this section you will find out how to make the most of your family home. Here are some brief suggestions that will be covered in greater detail in the pages that follow.

• Avoid contaminating your home with the chi of nasty arguments, simmering resentment or jealousy by discussing such issues outside the home.

• Better understand your family's dynamics by examining everyone's three ki numbers. Discover ways to bring in the missing chi, if one or more members are opposite in terms of the five elements.

• Find out simple ways to make the chi more yin and peaceful, reducing the risk of arguments occurring.

• Increase the chi in your home that helps everyone to have fun and feel more playful.

• Focus on the kitchen, often the heart of the family home.

• Keep the chi of the utility rooms clean and functional.

• Make sure your storage is well organized so that everything has its place and the most-used items are accessible.

• The atmosphere of the nursery influences how your baby will sleep, along with the visual stimulation that he or she will receive, so it is important to set up this room carefully to increase the chances of a peaceful night.

Ideal children's spaces are ones where you can lie on the floor and the room is designed to be interesting at their height.

• Being part of a family means that at some point you are likely to suffer the loss of someone close to you.

Your home can play its part in preserving his or her memory and can make it easier to process all the emotions that go with bereavement.

• The living room tends to be a space where the family relaxes together, so it is helpful if the chi there supports this.

• The fabrics in a room provide softness, colour and sometimes imagery. Items such as sofas, chairs, beanbags, cushions, curtains and rugs tend to accumulate chi, just as they collect dust, so it helps to keep them clean.

• Children's playrooms are important for their development and it is helpful if children can spend time amid natural, living chi to encourage good emotional and physical health.

MAKE THE PERFECT ENVIRONMENT

BENEFIT Creates a good environment for the whole family

Your home is the place where the whole family comes together and merges their chi. How harmoniously this happens can be affected by the ambient chi of your home. If the chi moves too quickly, you may experience disruptions and find it hard to settle down together; too much vertical chi and you may not interact much at all.

The ideal is a fairly constant, even flow of chi with a strong horizontal component that encourages everyone to feel harmonious together. If there is slightly more downward chi, families generally find it easier to feel settled.

What you do

1 Sit comfortably on your own and think carefully about what is needed to improve your family life. For example, this might be spending more time together, being more accepting of each other, having more fun, being more appreciative or more respectful of each other's space and life journey.

2 Look through the nine types of chi on page 36 or at the chart on pages 37–41, to see which direction would bring in the kind of chi you all need more of. For example, northern chi helps give each other more space; western chi encourages everyone to be more playful; and north-western chi helps people to be more respectful towards each other.

3 Once you have identified the chi you want more of, try to incorporate its colours, materials, shapes or special feng shui features into your home. For instance, to bring in more western chi you could use the colour pink, metal objects, round shapes and some pink flowers in a silver vase.

4 Try turning your beds so that the tops of your heads point in the direction of the chi you need more of; or sit facing this direction more often. For example, to create a closer, more caring, stable family atmosphere, try absorbing more south-western chi.

Directional qualities

• **East** Being active and doing things; moving on quickly from disputes and getting on with life.

• **South-east** Being sensitive to each other, avoiding confrontations and seeking harmony.

• **South** Going out more and spending less time at home; being expressive and interactive at home.

• **South-west** Feeling closer and more dependent on each other; increasing the caring, sharing, sympathetic side of people.

• **West** Having more fun together, being playful and feeling content with each other.

• **North-west** Showing greater respect for each other, acting with greater dignity and being responsible towards other family members.

• **North** Giving each other more space and getting on with your own thing; being more accepting and affectionate, but independent.

• **North-east** Being clearer and more direct with each other. Not accepting situations that you are not happy with.

AVOID CONTAMINATING YOUR HOME WITH UPSETS

BENEFIT Keeps the atmosphere free of argumentative chi

Whenever you have a family argument, upset or violent disagreement, you project the chi associated with the emotions of the time into the space around you. Similarly if you are processing strong emotions, a simmering resentment, jealousy or anger, you radiate this chi into your immediate environment. If any of this happens while you are at home, the risk is that you will fill your home with this chi. If this happens on a regular basis, it will have a cumulative effect, with the result that you could feel those emotions each time you go home as you pick up on some of the residual chi from the last upset.

What you do

• If you want to discuss a sensitive issue that you know will potentially provoke a strong reaction, if you want to express something that you feel strongly about, or if you sense that something is coming to a head, arrange to work through it all somewhere outside your home. A park, café, bar or public building means that your home will not become contaminated by the chi of the interaction and you will not acquire negative associations.

• If you do have an argument at home, try to clear out the chi soon afterwards by opening the windows. If necessary, you can sprinkle sea salt on the floor in the evening, then vacuum it up and throw it out of your home the next morning.

• A general clean-up and tidy will help stir up and move on any negative chi from the previous day and refresh the atmosphere.

When you need to have a potentially confrontational discussion, do it out of your home to avoid contaminating the chi there. Sitting to one side of each other like this is less confrontational than sitting opposite each other.

FAMILY FENG SHUI ASTROLOGY

> **BENEFIT** A better understanding of family relationships

By analyzing the feng shui astrology chi of each member of a family you get an impression of how everyone fits together. You might find that some children relate more closely to their father and others to their mother, providing useful information on who should best help him or her through difficulties. In some cases one child may be very different from the rest of the family, making it a little harder for him or her to fit in and feel included.

What you do

1 Look up everyone's three numbers on page 44, then look at page 36 to see which element is associated with each number. For example, the number 1 is associated with water. Write each person's name, their three numbers and the associated elements below the respective numbers.

2 Using the five-element diagram on page 30, work through each family member's numbers to see who shares the same element, which members have elements that are next to each other and which have opposites. You need to compare only the numbers in the same positions. For example, compare the year number with other year numbers, then compare the month number with other month numbers, and finally compare the axis numbers with other axis numbers. The year number describes how family members get on in the long term, the month numbers how they interact emotionally, and the axis numbers how they play together.

EXAMPLE OF A FAMILY CHART

YEAR	MONTH	AXIS
Person A		
Metal	Wood	Soil
7	4	8
Person B		
Metal	Metal	Metal
7	6	6

In this example, the year numbers are the same, the month numbers are opposites, and the axis numbers are harmonious.

3 Identify those members who share an element. They will find it easier to understand each other, even if they do not agree.

4 Identify the family members who have elements next to each other. This suggests a harmonious relationship where there is give and take.

5 Identify the members who have elements that are opposite each other. They will enjoy a dynamic relationship with great attraction, but will find it harder to understand each other.

BRING IN THE MISSING CHI

> **BENEFIT** Makes the family closer

You may find, when looking at your family as a whole, that everyone is connected to someone else in terms of the same element or an element that is harmonious (see page 284). If this is the case, the family often achieves some kind of balance, where problems are worked out with the intervention of another member. For example, if two siblings have month numbers with the elements of fire and water, there is a risk of misunderstandings occurring; however, another family member with a month number associated with the wood element could bridge the gap and find it easier to bring about a satisfactory resolution.

In some families one member might be out on his or her own, in terms of the five elements, with nobody having the same element or one next to his or hers. This can lead to feelings of exclusion, being different and not fitting in.

What you do

1 In a situation where one family member is opposite everyone else, look at the five-element chart on page 30 to see which element to bring in to bridge the gap. For example, soil chi brings harmony to fire and metal.

2 Use colours, materials and shapes around your home from the element that bridges the gap. For instance, yellows, beiges, browns and matt black bring in more soil chi. Fabrics, clay and earthenware products further increase it. Low, flat shapes bring more soil chi into a room.

EXAMPLE OF A FAMILY CHART WITH A MISSING ELEMENT

YEAR	MONTH	AXIS	YEAR	MONTH	AXIS
Mother			**Brother**		
Soil	Soil	Soil	Soil	Fire	Metal
2	2	5	2	9	7
Father			**Sister**		
Metal	Fire	Soil	Wood	Water	Metal
6	9	2	3	1	7

In this example, the sister's year and month chi are opposite those of the rest of her family.

3 If you feel there is enough of a problem to warrant it, try turning the bed of the family member in question so that the top of his or her head points in a direction that provides chi with the missing element. In the example used here, pointing south-west or north-east would bring in more soil chi.

REDUCE ARGUMENTS

BENEFIT Calms the atmosphere by changing the mix of chi present

One way to help reduce tension at home is to create a more yin, quiet atmosphere where chi moves more slowly. This makes it easier not to react in the moment and to consider what you say more carefully. It is helpful to build a home where chi does not bounce around, but moves peacefully through each room.

What you do

1 Make the atmosphere more yin using soft natural fabrics, for instance on big cushions, full-length curtains and tablecloths. Pale blues, greens and cream colours further help everyone to relax. Avoid bright colours, particularly red or purple, as this could add more fiery, potentially argumentative chi.

2 Soften any sharp corners with bushy plants or natural fabrics to reduce your family's exposure to fast, spinning chi.

3 To make the atmosphere quieter, bring in more northern chi energy. This is associated with the night and winter. Use cream colours, flowing shapes and glass – for example, cream flowers in a curvy glass vase. If anyone is consistently tense, try seating them so that they face north. Other relaxing directions to face are west, north-west and south-west.

4 Be aware that the fiery, potentially explosive chi energy of the south will aggravate the situation. Keep charcoal in a clay container in the southern part of your home, as soil chi calms the fire chi of the south. Also use pale yellows, beiges or browns, and soft furnishings in the south, to further calm the fire chi there.

5 Grow bushy or floppy-leafed plants to bring in more yin, peaceful chi. Move any spiky-leafed plants so that they are well away from anywhere your family sits or tries to relax.

6 Review the number of mirrors you have and see if you can reduce them so that the chi in your home is not reflected back and forth.

Shaded lighting and soft fabrics (both soil chi) along with yin cream colours make this a calm, peaceful space where it will be easier to settle differences.

HAVE FUN TOGETHER

> **BENEFIT** Creates a more playful atmosphere

To give your home a more fun atmosphere you need to increase the presence of western chi. This more playful energy is associated with the sunset, the trigram of the youngest daughter, the lake and harvest time. As you take in more of this chi, you should feel the sense of joy you get when you finish a day's work with an evening of fun ahead of you.

What you do

1 To build up western chi try using the colour pink. This will be most effective in the west part of your home. Keep pink flowers here – for example, a pair of roses in a silver vase.

2 To absorb more western chi, sleep with the top of your head pointing west or sit facing this direction more often.

3 Make your home slightly more yin. Pastel colours, soft furnishings and curved shapes will all help. Straight lines, sharp corners and an over-regimented furniture layout will make the atmosphere too yang and serious. Use plants to soften any sharp edges and to break up some of the straight lines.

4 Keep romantic pictures, sculptures and poems in places where you will see them often. Try playing more romantic music at the appropriate times.

5 Check on page 53 to see which phase your year number is in this year, and in which month it will be in the west. It will be easiest to have fun when your year number is to the west, south-east or south.

Wearing pink brings more western chi into your own chi field helping you feel more playful.

6 Hang a mirror in the west so that its back faces an outside wall, as this will activate the flow of western chi here.

7 Clothes that include the colour pink or red, silver jewellery and soft fabrics will surround you with more fun, playful chi.

KITCHEN AND DINING AREA

BENEFIT Strengthens the heart of the family

The kitchen and dining areas often form the heart of a family, because these are the places where everyone comes together for food and drink. For many families with older children, this is the main meeting place. The atmosphere here is important so that when you do all come together, it is a high-quality experience and helps build positive associations for everyone. To make this work well it is ideal to create a fairly contained chi that is slow-moving and settled. This is primarily defined by the soil chi of the south-west and metal chi of the west.

What you do

1 Use wood in the areas you want to spend most time in, as this will be more yin than stone or metal. If you want to slow the chi further and make it easier to spend more time together, try putting cushions on the chairs, using cotton or linen tablecloths and laying a rug on the floor.

2 To bring in more settled soil chi, use the colours yellow, brown, beige or orange. These could be used in your cushions, tablecloth, napkins, placemats or crockery.

3 To help contain the chi in the eating area, try using more metal, circular shapes. A round or oval table will make it easier for everyone to see each other and communicate, keeping the chi of the family at the table.

4 Bring the chi down by keeping the lighting close to the floor while you eat. Turn off overhead lights and rely either on table lamps with fabric shades or candles.

Keep materials soft and natural if you want to create the best atmosphere to get together. Wood, linen and earthenware are ideal.

UTILITY ROOM

> **BENEFIT** Cleaner chi

It is important to keep any room that processes water harmonious with
the ambient chi, so that the passage of water through the room happens
smoothly. Any kind of water chi generated in a utility room by a sink or
washing machine mixes with the chi of that part of your home. This mixing
can be made harmonious using the five-element theory (see page 30).
The principle is to add more of the chi between the two opposite elements.
In addition, should there be too much water chi in one place, this can be
drained away. Alternatively, if the water chi is draining away the ambient chi,
this chi can be strengthened.

What you do

• A utility room in the north risks an excess of water chi, making it more
likely that family members will worry, feel lonely or isolated. This will need to
be drained with more wood chi, in the form of plants, wooden surfaces and
the colour green.

• The soil chi of the north-east, south-west or centre can have a destructive
influence on water chi, causing a loss of vitality, poor health and a reduced
sex drive. Harmonize the water and soil chi with more metal chi. This can be
achieved using more metal surfaces, round shapes, tiles and the colours
silver or grey.

• If your utility room is to the south, the water chi can potentially destroy the
fire chi there, making it harder to be sociable, passionate or expressive,
unless there is sufficient wood chi energy. Add plenty of plants, wooden
surfaces or objects and the colour green.

• Should your utility room be sited to the west or north-west, the water chi can have a draining influence on the metal chi, risking a lack of financial awareness, pleasure or romance. To reinforce the metal chi, use more metal surfaces, round shapes, tiles and the colours silver or grey.

A window in your utility room is a huge bonus as it lets in fresh chi.

STORAGE

> **BENEFIT** Better organization

Having proper, functional storage means that you can keep open surfaces clean and clear, so the chi moves more easily. It is also more practical if you know exactly where everything is, saving hours of looking for things. When storing objects, it is important to make your storage as functional as possible. Everything needs to be accessible, out of the way, easy to clean and good to look at. You need to match all the items you want to store with the space that you have available.

What you do

1 Put everything you need to store in the middle of your room and sort it out into the way you want to store it, how often you need it and where it should be (for example, hanging space, shelving or boxes). Some things will need to be in your bedroom, bathroom or kitchen.

2 When storing, decide whether it would help to be able to see the items through glass doors or in jars, or whether you need to label the containers.

3 Try to use freestanding storage units as much as possible so that you leave yourself the option to change the room around at a later date. This more flexible approach also makes it easier to adapt to your changing needs as the years go by.

4 For long-term storage, you can use your loft or garage. Even though these place are often out of sight, it is still important to invest in proper storage systems so that you can find everything when you need it.

5 To increase the chi that helps you feel more organized at home, clear out the north-west part of your house or apartment. You can increase the chi here using plants in metal containers, or hang a pendulum clock with as many metal parts as possible to bring a greater sense of rhythm and structure to your home. This is

Freestanding storage units give you the flexibility to move things around when you want to create a different mood.

important because you still need to be able to maintain your storage system and keep everything in its right place, once you have finished sorting it.

LIVING ROOM

BENEFIT Getting more of the chi you need

The decor and design of your living room define the overall chi of the room and you can make this more yin or yang with colours, patterns, materials and the amount of furniture you put there. When arranging the chairs in your living room you also have the opportunity to place yourself and your family in positions that can help you feel the way you want to.

One of the most powerful influences will be the direction you face, but this is not the only consideration. It is also good practice to sit so that your back is protected by a wall, screen or big plant, and to have as much of the room as possible open in front of you. If several people use this room, the chairs need to be arranged to bring out a good social atmosphere. Generally, having the chairs facing the centre of the room will help to achieve this.

What you do

1 To work out which direction you are facing, sit holding your compass so that the body faces away from you, and note the reading.

2 Decide which direction from the list below best suits your needs and then arrange your furniture accordingly.

Placing chairs on a rug slows the flow of chi around the chairs, making the area a little more settled, cosy and comfortable.

Directional qualities

• **East** Advantageous for being active, ambitious and busy; ideal for putting ideas into practice.

• **South-east** Favourable for communication; beneficial if you want to have a good talk.

• **South** Useful for feeling passionate, expressive and sociable; ideal for entertaining friends.

• **South-west** Associated with long-term relationships and beneficial for family harmony.

• **West** Ideal for romance, pleasure, feeling more content and settling down at sunset.

• **North-west** Best for taking care of your family's needs and making decisions with greater wisdom.

• **North** Useful for feeling quieter, more peaceful and tranquil; helpful for meditation.

• **North-east** Beneficial for motivation, feeling a sense of direction and being more competitive.

SEATING

> **BENEFIT** Feeling settled, comfortable and cosy

Soft furnishings in general slow down chi, making the whole space feel softer, more cosy and comfortable. And the shape of your seating defines what posture you adopt when sitting in them. The closer to the floor you are, the greater your connection with the chi of the earth. This soil chi tends to help you feel secure and stable, so lying on a big cushion or beanbag brings you closer to it.

In addition, the more upright you are, the more vertical and yang your chi flow is; the closer you are to lying down, the more yin and relaxed you feel. In general, try to introduce a variety of seating into a room so that you have the option to adopt different postures according to your moods. Each posture changes the shape of your outer chi field, helping you to feel and think differently.

Another consideration is whether a chair supports you in terms of the five animals (see page 34). For this you need a tall back, with full support for your arms.

*Sitting close to the floor in a
reclined position helps you
connect with a more settled chi,
making it easier to feel content.*

What you do

1 Look around your living room and make a mental note of the different types of seating.

2 See if there is any form of seating that gives you the option to adopt postures that will better suit your moods. Most people already have armchairs and sofas, so you need to consider other forms of seating, such as straight-backed chairs, beanbags or big cushions on the floor.

3 Work out how you could introduce other forms of seating so that you can still be placed in an empowering position within the room. For example, it helps to have your back to a wall with a view of the door and windows. In addition, you could check to see if you will face a direction that brings you more of the chi you desire.

NURSERY

> **BENEFIT** Healthy sleep

A baby spends a considerable part of the day asleep, and good-quality sleep is essential to healthy growth. The prime function of a nursery is therefore to provide the ideal environment for sound sleep.

The location of your baby's bed within a room will affect his or her sleeping patterns – particularly the direction in which the top of the head points, as this will determine which chi your baby absorbs more of during the night. It will also have an influence during the day.

What you do

Look at the directions below and choose the one you think will most help your baby.

• **East** Ideal for growth, making this direction helpful for a child at the beginning of life. As the energy of the east is most active at the start of the day, it also helps in terms of feeling bright in the morning.

• **South-east** Helpful for sleep, along with harmonious growth and development; this direction tends to stimulate your baby's imagination and creativity.

• **South** Could result in poor sleep; the advantage is that it helps to develop quick thinking and a spontaneous spirit.

• **South-west** A settled position, which encourages good sleep; this chi promotes a cautious, practical and caring nature.

• **West** Combines the benefits of good sleep with a playful, joyful, contented atmosphere.

• **North-west** A more serious kind of chi and probably too mature for a baby, although it does help in terms of sleep and wisdom.

• **North** A quiet direction, which can help a baby who finds it difficult to sleep; it is best to use north temporarily, as this chi is too still for a growing child.

• **North-east** Too hard and piercing for good sleep – it could even make your child more prone to tantrums; this is an energy that would only be helpful if you think your baby could be more motivated and competitive.

If you notice that your baby turns in his sleep, check the compass direction in which the top of his head points in order to find out which chi he wants more of.

CHILDREN'S ROOM

BENEFIT A more natural childhood

The ideal atmosphere in a children's room is one that encourages a full night's sleep, but also has chi that is supportive to growing, developing children. Apart from sleep, this room may also be used as a playroom, which introduces the challenge of making the room fun during the day and peaceful at night. If you have sufficient space, however, it is better to use separate rooms for sleep and play.

The more natural the atmosphere in your children's room, the easier it will be for them to feel relaxed, which can lead to better sleep and behaviour. There is a risk that artificial materials will give off fumes and build up a charge of static electricity, potentially compromising your child's health.

What you do

1 Try to make your children aware of the materials that their toys are made of, and encourage them to choose those made of metal, wood or fabric rather than plastic.

2 Move any electric items, such as computers, lights, wires or heaters, well away from their beds. If possible, take them out of the bedroom altogether and use another room, as your children will be more susceptible to EMF while they are in bed.

3 Check the fabrics in your children's bedroom, include their clothing, bedding, curtains, carpet, rugs and cushions. If these contain synthetic fibres, replace them with something made from pure cotton or linen. The closer something is to your child's skin, the greater its influence on their chi energy field. Most important are underclothes, pyjamas and sheets.

4 If you are short of space, you could use a futon instead of a bed, which can be rolled up and tucked away during the daytime to create a larger play area.

5 Avoid furniture made from MDF or veneered wood, as these could add toxic fumes to the room. Try always to use solid wood, as this is a much better conductor of chi energy.

6 Grow several healthy plants in the room.

Keep the materials in your child's room as natural as possible to avoid the build up of toxic fumes.

BEREAVEMENT: BUILDING A SACRED SHRINE

BENEFIT A greater sense of completion

When someone close to you dies, it is natural to go through feelings of loss, loneliness, grief, fear, depression or anger. One way to try and preserve a spiritual connection with a loved one who has passed away is to build a shrine for him or her.

This will help you feel that you have a specific place dedicated to that person. This can become your special space in which to think about your loved one – a place to talk to him or her, and somewhere you can relive some of the happy memories.

What you do

1 Choose a site in the north-west or north part of your home or room. The site should be somewhere you can put a table, shelf or stand.

2 Select photos of your loved one that remind you of your happiest times together. You could create a visual story of his or her journey through life, with pictures of your loved one as a child, through all the important events,

until close to the end of his or her life. This can help put everything into perspective.

3 Place the photographs on the table, shelf or stand, and add a bowl of fresh water, a plant or fresh flowers, a small bowl of raw whole grains (such as brown rice), a candle and a small dish of sea salt. Change the water daily and the salt and grain weekly.

Place items that remind you of your loved one on a table or shelf so that this space becomes a shrine where you can feel close to them.

4 If you are creating this shine for someone who died many years ago, you can visit his or her grave to bring back a stone from close to the burial site and put it in the bowl of water.

5 When you feel like it, light the candle and kneel or sit looking at your shrine. Here you can relive some of your time together and talk about anything that you feel has been left unsaid.

FENG SHUI AND YOUR CAREER

THE HOME OFFICE

The home office is becoming an increasingly important feature of modern home life, as more people have the opportunity – and the desire – to work from home. Many companies now offer the option for employees to do some of their work from home.

This has become possible because computers, e-mail connections, the Internet, telephones, fax machines, copiers and scanners now mean that even the smallest office can operate globally. The problem with most home offices is that they tend to be small, and the person working there is exposed to potentially high levels of EMF. However, there are many ways to improve your home office using feng shui. The following ideas represent the essence of creating the home office, and are covered in greater detail later in this section.

• One of the main issues is to find the best place to sit. It is most important to immerse yourself in the best chi, in order to be able to work to your full potential.

• Your work station defines how you interface with your work, as well as influencing the way you feel there. Because modern ways of working have changed so much, there is a greater need for new types of desk to make everything work efficiently.

• The chair you sit on is vital to your comfort and the long-term health of your back, shoulders and neck.

• EMF from all the electrical equipment in a modern office can reduce your ability to think clearly and concentrate – in extreme situations it may even contribute to a long-term health problem.

• Ideally every time you walk into your office you will feel inspired, so it is important to get the imagery right for you.

• Whenever you have important phases in your career, you can use feng shui astrology to try and get the timing right. This is helpful if you have a five- or ten-year plan and can think ahead. For the short term, you can find the ideal phase in the coming nine months.

• Each month and year various directions become favourable to you, based on your year number. This can help you focus your efforts more clearly on the best directions from your home for finding new work.

When working with another person, sitting at an angle to each other brings your outer chi fields together in a harmonious way.

CREATE A LAUNCH PAD FOR YOUR CAREER

> **BENEFIT** Starting a new career or boosting an old one

So much of your adult life may be spent at work that it makes a vast difference if you are doing something you enjoy and believe in. When it's all going well, your career can be a huge source of inspiration and can even give you more energy. To help make this happen, your home office should be the launch pad for the career you really want.

To successfully start a new career you need enthusiasm, confidence and the belief that you can make it happen. These qualities are found in the chi energy of the east. To help you get off to the best start, you need to bring more eastern chi into your own energy field. This chi will also help you boost and activate an existing career that is not quite where you want it to be.

What you do

1 Place a bowl in the east part of your home or office. Refill the bowl each morning so that you bring more fresh-water energy there. Water is supportive to the wood energy of the east and increases the presence of this morning, springtime energy. This will be more powerful if it is possible to position the water so that the morning sun hits it.

2 Grow plants in the east part of your office to increase the eastern chi – the plants also represent wood chi and bring in more of that energy.

3 Work facing east so that you can directly bring this energy into your own chi field. If this is not possible, try facing south-east.

4 To start something new, clear the decks for action. Get rid of everything you no longer need and make the space for something new to happen. It is harder to start something when you are cramped for space and still surrounded by clutter from previous projects.

Sitting up high in an open uncluttered space makes it easier to be clear-minded, decisive and focused.

SITTING POSITIONS

> **BENEFIT** Absorbs the chi to improve your career

The direction in which you face aligns you with a particular chi, and this makes a difference to the way you work in your office.

What you do

Each direction is listed below, together with its potential benefits, so that you can choose the direction that is most favourable to you. You can also choose it according to the kind of work you do, although this is a secondary priority. The position of your desk in relationship to the doors and windows has a significant influence on the way you feel in your office. In the case of the door, it also influences the way in which you are perceived by other people, should you have visitors to your office. Ideally the door should be forward of your desk.

Directional benefits

• **East** Promotes activity, ambition and confidence; favourable for activities relating to computers, business start-ups and information technology.

• **South-east** Promotes creativity, communication and persistence; favourable for activities relating to communication, marketing, distribution, travel and creativity.

• **South** Promotes quick thinking, the ability to be noticed and expressiveness; favourable for activities relating to sales, PR, marketing and entertainment.

• **South-west** Promotes improving quality, consolidation and practicality; favourable for activities relating to human resources, buildings, customer services and team-building.

• **West** Promotes financial awareness, the ability to complete tasks and contentment; favourable for activities relating to finance, accounts and investments.

Flat screens give you more space and allow you to move the screen further away from you, reducing your exposure to EMF.

• **North-west** Promotes organization, leadership qualities and responsibility; favourable for activities relating to management, administration and forward planning.

• **North** Promotes objectivity, calmness and flexibility; favourable for activities relating to self-development, training and cashflow.

• **North-east** Promotes hard work, motivation and a competitive attitude; favourable for activities relating to competition, purchasing, trading and buildings.

THE OFFICE DESK

> **BENEFIT** Efficient working

The most immediate influence on you while you are at work is your desk. It not only defines how you work, but also the way you feel when you work, influencing your own chi and therefore the way you think while at your desk. The material that the desk is made of, its shape, size and the way you arrange objects on it all have an influence on you.

What you do

• Curved worktops create a more natural appearance and reduce the risk of generating sharp, spinning chi from corners.

• A large desk with a big, clear open space to work on will help you feel better able to take on more work without getting stressed. In the long term it will help you be more ambitious. Generally, keeping your desktop clear of clutter and your storage spaces well organized will help you work efficiently.

• A solid wooden desk provides a material that is conducive to a natural flow of chi. Desks that are made of woodchips, or wood dust bonded with adhesives, tend to block the flow of chi, in a similar way to plastic. These materials are usually covered with a thin veneer of real wood.

• Darker hardwoods (such as mahogany) are more yang, and create the appearance of a more imposing, formal and serious office. Lighter softwoods (such as pine) are more yin, and bring in relaxed, casual chi to your energy field.

• A glass-topped desk speeds up the flow of chi across its surface, making it a more spontaneous place at which to work. However, this more yang surface is not supportive if you wish to work there for long periods of time.

The glass surface encourages a faster flow of chi, helping you work quickly. This would not be good when you need to be patient and careful.

THE OFFICE CHAIR

BENEFIT Good posture

As you can spend so much time sitting in a chair in front of a computer, it is essential that your office chair is designed to be comfortable over long periods. One of the causes of back, neck and shoulder pain is your posture while seated at work.

The base of the spine needs to be angled correctly so that the upper body is balanced over your lumbar vertebrae, in such a way that the muscles

along the spine (including those of the neck) do not have to compensate for poor posture. The risk is that, as these muscles get tired and overworked, they become sore. During the process of correcting poor posture, the muscles build up lactic acids, which in turn lead to stiffness. If these muscles are subjected to this same regime on a regular basis, there is a risk of long-term pain and stiffness. Stiff muscles are more susceptible to injury, and many backaches are due to a pulled muscle going into spasm. This greatly restricts your mobility and can result in severe pain and loss of mobility.

To reduce these risks, use a chair that has the ability to tilt the seat. By adjusting the angle of the seat, it is possible to maintain the optimum angle for your lumbar vertebrae, so that your back, shoulders and neck are positioned over the base of your spine. In addition the chair needs to be adjustable for height. In most situations, it is helpful to have a chair that is on castors, for ease of movement.

What you do

1 Set the seat base so that it is level.

2 Adjust the height so that your feet are flat on the floor while the underside of your upper legs is gently supported by the seat.

3 Tip the seat forward slowly until you just feel your lower back tilt into a position where you do not need to lean back.

4 Adjust the height of the seat again, if necessary.

Try to get an office chair that is adjustable in height and has a seat that tilts so you can maintain the ideal posture.

WORKING WITH COMPUTERS AND REDUCING EMF

BENEFIT Better concentration, mental clarity and long-term health

Everything that uses or transports electricity produces an electromagnetic field or EMF. This is of particular concern in your office as so much modern equipment uses electricity. Some research suggests that exposure to EMF could be detrimental to your health, with increased risks ranging from headaches to cancer. EMF distorts the earth's natural magnetic field and is therefore undesirable in feng shui. From a feng shui perspective, exposure to EMF in your office will make it harder to concentrate, think clearly and remain enthused.

The best way to reduce your exposure to EMF is to keep as far away from the source of it as possible. Generally, the closer an electrical item is, the higher its voltage and the more electricity it uses, the greater your exposure to EMF.

What you do

1 Make a note of all the objects you have that are powered by electricity. See how close you are to them when sitting at your desk.

2 Unplug anything that you use infrequently, as this will ensure that the transformer is no longer live and emitting EMF.

3 Move electrical equipment so that it is as far from your office chair as possible. For example, see if you can arrange your office so that you are at least 1 m (3 ft) from any electrical equipment.

4 The central processing unit (CPU) of your computer can emit higher levels of EMF than the keyboard, and you should keep this further away from you. Similarly, see if you can move your computer screen so that it is further from you. A flat screen is ideal, as you will be able to move it further back and it should emit less radiation.

5 If you have a laptop, keep the remote transformer as far from you as possible.

6 Wherever possible, grow a peace lily, a spider plant or a South American cactus next to your computer, as this may help counter some of the effects of EMF (see page 142–143).

A plant on your desk may reduce the EMF from the computer and make the area feel more alive.

MAKE IT INSPIRING

BENEFIT Greater mental stimulation

The quality of your work depends on how you feel in your office. It is therefore helpful to fill your office with imagery that inspires you to work better. This could be achieved by reminders of things you have done well in the past, by images of something you aspire to, or by items that simply make you feel good.

What you do

1 Collect all the potential imagery that you might put in your office. These could be prints, paintings, models, toys, certificates, awards, sculptures or photographs.

2 Make a pile of those that inspire you. For example, if you've always wanted to visit Tuscany, you might choose a picture of a local Italian village; if you've always dreamt of owning an E-type Jaguar, you might keep a model of this classic car; or you could have a drawing of your ideal home.

3 Make another pile of objects that you know make you feel proud of yourself. This might include awards, reminders of jobs you have done really well, or something that recalls a time in your life when you felt really good about yourself.

4 Lastly, put together things that are guaranteed to make you feel more positive. This might be anything from paintings and photographs of people you love to sculptures, toys or clocks.

5 Select items from these three groups to go in your office. If possible, it will make a subtle difference if you put those things that inspire you in the east, south-east or south; those reminders from the past in the west, north-west or north; and those items

Use the wall space to display imagery that you find inspiring and helps drive you forward.

that make you feel positive in the south-west, west, north or north-east parts of your office.

TIME IMPORTANT CAREER CHANGES

BENEFIT Being more effective

You can use your natural cycles to try and find the time when the forces of nature will make it easier to do want you want, in terms of your career. Use the information below to make this happen. You will also need to look at pages 42, 44 and 53 to gather the information you require.

What you do

To start a new career

• **East** Represents confidence, enthusiasm and ambition, helping you get off to a good start and established quickly.

• **South-east** Represents a positive phase for taking on something new that can lead to future prosperity.

• **South** Good for making an impression and being noticed; you will find it easier to promote yourself and get job offers in this phase.

• **West** Symbolizes financial awareness; you may find that you can arrange terms that are lucrative for you.

• **North-west** Signifies dignity, responsibility and authority; ideal if you intend to take on a management role.

• **North-east** Symbolizes competitiveness and motivation – a phase that could make your career more stressful and prone to conflicts.

To ask for a rise

• **East and south-east** Represent positive phases in which to find another job, making you feel more confident about playing the field.

• **West** Increases your financial income, as this chi is associated with the harvest time and bringing money inwards.

• **North-west** Signifies dignity and wisdom to negotiate an improved salary.

To apply for promotion

• **South-east** A generally positive direction, when it is easier to make a harmonious transition into a more senior role.

• **South** Symbolizes a time to promote yourself, develop your reputation and attract attention.

• **North-west** Associated with leadership and an easier time to win respect and present yourself as able to take on extra responsibility.

• **North-east** Represents a chance to spot an opportunity and seize it quickly.

To start a business

• **East** Ideal for starting a new business and getting off to a flying start; the following phase (south-east) is also positive for growth, marketing and building up the business, giving you two years to get established.

• **West** Focuses on the end result and setting up in a way to maximize profits; followed by north-east and south, which help you to become competitive and receive public exposure respectively, giving you three years to get established.

BEST DIRECTION FOR YOUR CAREER AND BUSINESS

> **BENEFIT** Finding work and new clients

Each year certain directions become more favourable to you, depending on your year number (see pages 42, 44 and 58). In any year the directions that are most helpful to you make it easier to succeed, if you have to do something in that direction. For example, if you are looking for a new job, want to find new clients or set up a new business, it would be wise to find out which directions are helpful to you and then focus your efforts in that direction. In theory you will be able to achieve more with less effort, as you get a natural lift from the positive chi.

What you do

1 Find out which directions are best for you from the charts on pages 42, 44 and 58.

2 Get a map with your home on it and the surrounding area that is applicable to your career or business. Ideally this should all be on one page, or on a large-format folded or roll-out map.

3 Draw the eight directions on the map by placing the centre of your transparency over your home (see pages 112–115).

4 Look in those directions that are favourable to you in this year, to see if there are potential areas to find a new career or clients.

By choosing the direction that you face during work you can charge yourself with the best kind of chi for the work you do.

5 You can also check the following year, so that you are always prepared and looking ahead. Try using different-coloured 'sticky notes' to mark the favourable directions for different years, to avoid confusion.

6 To focus your energy more precisely, you can work out which months have favourable directions that coincide with those for the year, then see if you can target those times for your new job or business.

FENG SHUI AND NATURE

YOUR CONNECTION TO NATURE

Living in any home, even one with the best feng shui, will always be a compromise, as the internal environment is bound to be somewhat artificial. You can control the chi inside your home fairly easily, but inevitably you lose some of the living vitality that wild nature has to offer.

It is easier to bring more natural, living chi into your home if you live in the country or have a garden. This section looks at ways in which you can make the most of the chi around your home and get a better connection to nature, so that your energy field is fed by some of the chi from the plants, trees and wildlife close by. Here are some of the key elements in making a stronger connection with nature.

• Plants, flowers, wood, sunlight and fresh air fill your home with chi from outdoors.

• Window boxes create strong natural chi close to your windows, making it easier for this energy to enter your home.

• Balconies provide an excellent opportunity to create some living chi close to your home if you live in a residential area.

• Gardens enable you to bring nature close to your home, while at the same time you have an influence over the kind of chi found there.

• Outdoor water features bring healthy water chi close to your own energy field, making it easier to increase your vitality.

• Paths help to define the flow of chi through your garden, so you can design them in such a way that energy moves around and into your home.

• Sculptures and works of art enhance the imagery of your garden and set the scene for feeling inspired and uplifted.

• The trees and plants you choose to place around your home define the way chi from the heavens mixes with chi from the earth. This has a powerful effect on your own chi and therefore a major influence on your moods.

• A conservatory brings you closer to nature while you are still inside your home. For climates where you cannot spend all year in your garden, a conservatory is a helpful addition.

The nature around your home will enter through the doors, windows and, to a lesser extent, the walls influencing the internal chi.

CONNECT TO THE SOURCE OF VITALITY

BENEFIT Recharges your chi

Your own chi is dependent on outside chi to be replenished, revitalized and recharged. We need this mixing with outside forces to feel alive and stimulated, and it is therefore helpful to find ways to make this an active process.

The most obvious solution is to spend time outdoors in areas where you feel that nature is vibrant and alive. Once there, you can find ways to absorb the natural chi around you.

What you do

1 Look for opportunities to get out into natural environments. This might be a park, a field, a picnic spot or just a small grassy square with a few trees.

2 Once you have found your natural spot, certain activities will help you absorb more of the chi around you. Having a picnic means that you are in the process of taking chi into your body through your food, and you will find that at the same time you take in some of the surrounding chi.

3 Sunbathing and feeling the fresh air and sun on your bare skin makes it possible to take in more natural chi. This can be deeply relaxing and is the most effective way to absorb some of the solar chi from the centre of our solar system – the sun. Due to the damage done to the ozone layer, you will need to be careful about how much exposure to direct sunlight you have. Mornings and evenings are safest if you have sensitive skin.

4 Relaxing and thinking about deeper issues in your life will help you soak up some of the chi around you, whereas talking and being active will project your own chi more strongly.

Being outside most strongly connects you with nature's chi. See if you can make time to plant yourself in this life-giving energy.

BRING NATURE INTO YOUR HOME

BENEFIT Greater natural chi in your home

To increase the natural chi in your home – and therefore your exposure to natural chi while you are at home – you need to find ways to bring in more elements that contain and emit chi, along with increasing your exposure to outside forces.

In reality this means bringing in more plants and fresh flowers, and exposing your home to plenty of fresh air and sunlight. A more subtle addition would be the use of wood, as this still contains some living chi.

What you do

1 Bring as many natural healthy plants into your home as possible. Try to get a variety and to create small gardens by putting a mixture of plants in the same large pot. If you are adventurous, you may be able to create a small indoor rockery in a part of your home. Remember that you can use plants growing in pots, hanging plants and vines to make the most of the available space.

2 Open your windows regularly to let fresh air through your home. Do this while you are performing

Experiment with plants on the floor, on furniture, hanging in baskets and vines to fill your home with living chi.

any kind of cleaning, so that you mix the fresh chi with the dormant chi of your home more effectively.

3 Encourage sunlight to come into your home. This is easiest with east- or west-facing windows, as the sun is lower in the sky and will penetrate right into your home.

4 Wherever possible, use bare wood so that you can bring in more living chi in surfaces or furniture. If you need to protect the wood, use a natural wax rather than varnish or lacquer, which tends to encapsulate the wood in a material that does not allow chi to flow easily.

WINDOW BOXES

BENEFIT Brings natural chi close to your home

Window boxes are an excellent way to bring natural, colourful chi close to your home. This is particularly useful as window boxes enhance the chi entering your home through its windows. This is a great asset if you live in an apartment building in a city, where you are fairly removed from nature.

You can choose the colours of the flowers according to the kind of chi energy you wish to increase and the direction that the front of your home faces. Stronger colours bring in more stimulating yang chi, while pale colours generate more peaceful yin chi.

If you can, choose a variety of flowers so that something is in flower for as much of the year as possible. In addition, consider growing herbs in your window boxes, because they will emit fragrances and be a healthy source of nutrients in your cooking.

What you do

Use the direction from the centre of your home in which you intend to fix your window box to help you decide which material to use. Place your eight-directions transparency over the centre of your floor plan (see pages 112–115) and align it with north, so that you can see in which direction the appropriate window lies.

The pink, red and white flowers bring more western chi into this home through the windows helping people inside feel more content.

• A metal window box is best in the south-west, north-east, west, north-west or north.

• A wooden window box is best in the north, east, south-east or south.

• An earthenware window box is best in the south, south-west, north-east, west or north-west.

• Avoid using plastic window boxes, as they can disrupt the flow of energy.

BALCONIES

BENEFIT Brings in fresh, living chi

The prime advantages of a balcony are that you often get good views from them and great exposure to sunshine. Being able to tap into this open chi is a great boon. You can further enhance this by creating a small garden on your balcony. This colours the chi coming into your home, giving it a different feel.

One helpful aspect of creating a garden on your balcony is that in summer you will have extra foliage, creating natural shade, while in winter this foliage will recede, leaving you free to get maximum exposure to the available winter sunlight.

In addition, spending time on your balcony will expose you to open, free-moving chi. You should find this inspiring, stimulating to your imagination and helpful for free thinking. The same applies to a roof garden.

What you do

1 Decide what kind of chi you need more of, and then plan your balcony to bring more of this chi into your home. For example, if you want greater yang stimulation, use colourful flowering plants, plants with spiky leaves and interesting containers. For a more yin, soft, calm feel, try plants with floppy leaves, vines and trellises.

2 Bear in mind that wooden decking will create a softer, yin chi compared to concrete or stone flooring. Similarly, wooden furniture will be more yin than metal chairs and tables.

3 You can add a point of interest by having a water feature or birdbath on your balcony. This would be best if your balcony faces east or south-east from the centre of your home.

Spending time on this balcony would place you close to the chi of the flowers.

GARDENS

BENEFIT Surrounds your home with vibrant chi

By creating the garden of your dreams, you can surround your home with the chi that helps you feel inspired and tranquil at the same time. Moreover, by going out into your garden, you can immerse yourself in this chi.

If your garden is large enough, you can create different atmospheres in different parts, so that you can soak up various types of chi according to your mood. For instance, open spaces encourage chi to move quickly, while small enclosed spaces contain the chi better.

What you do

1 See if there is an area that naturally lends itself to a more open environment. This would be the ideal space for a lawn. Think of this as a free-moving space where the chi will be more dynamic.

2 Look for a part of your garden where you can create a more enclosed space with vegetation, trees and bushes. Here the chi will be more contained, making it easier to relax and feel settled. This would be a good spot for a seat.

3 Think about creating an area where the chi will rise strongly. Here you need to plant trees, bamboos, tall wild grasses or any plants that grow up strongly.

4 Consider a space for a rockery, where you will be able to encourage clear, sharp chi, making you feel decisive and clear-headed.

5 Remember that shrubs, large-leafed tropical plants and paths help chi move horizontally, making it easier to feel sociable and to connect with other people.

6 Note that a rectangular garden with a central lawn and flower beds around the edges will be clearly laid out and accessible, leading to a more yang flow of chi. The more intricate your garden design is, with winding paths, hidden love nests and curved flower beds, the more yin its chi flow is.

The hard stone steps make a yang contrast to the yin foliage in this garden.

WATER FEATURES

> **BENEFIT** Increases vitality and freshness

Water that forms a part of your local landscape has an effect on the chi energy of your home. When the conditions are favourable, water has the ability to increase your vitality. A water feature brings more movement into your garden, creating a more active flow of chi. Whereas metal chi represents money, moving water chi is associated with the movement of money.

What you do

• All water should be clean, fresh and unpolluted. Water that becomes stagnant creates more stagnant chi energy, which, if close enough to you, could make your own chi stagnant.

• Moving water creates more yang chi than still water. For example, a waterfall has a more active yang influence than a pond. But the downward movement of a waterfall has a more grounding effect, as opposed to the uplifting chi of a bubbling spring.

• Fast-flowing water that moves in a straight line has a more yang influence than slow-moving water that meanders through gentle curves. Ponds and bogs have the most yin influence, but here it is important that there is a wide variety of thriving wildlife in order to avoid stagnation.

• The direction in which the water lies from the centre of your home also has an influence. It is most beneficial to have water located to the east or south-east, where it will help build up the wood chi of these directions.

• Water that flows towards the main entrance of your home has a greater ability to bring chi energy into your home, while water flowing away from the

entrance can diminish the chi energy inside your home. It could even lead to the feeling that money is flowing away from you.

Moving water stirs up the chi creating a more dynamic local atmosphere. Waterfalls also oxygenate the water giving it more vitality.

PATHS AND SCULPTURES

> **BENEFIT** Alters the flow of chi

Paths affect the appearance of your garden and the tactile experience of using it. When you choose the material for a path, you need to think what it would feel like to walk along each surface. Having a variety of surfaces will make your garden feel more interesting. A path made from a hard flat surface (such as paving stones) encourages chi to move faster. A straight path moves the chi faster still.

When planning a garden, use statues to emphasize an area. For instance, a statue in the middle of a circle draws attention to that area. A statue can also complete a view – a statue at the end of a path defines what that path leads to. Sometimes you can even use a statue to create a surprise: you could partially hide a statue among plants, or it could suddenly come into view as you round a corner.

The imaginative use of materials in this garden makes for a more interesting design.

The effect on chi of different materials

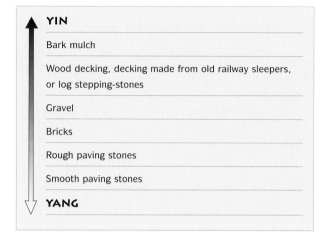

What you do

• To increase the romance in your life, place a romantic statue on a round base made of metal, surrounded by red flowers, in the west.

• To strengthen the chi energy associated with your career, put a tall wooden statue surrounded by green plants in the east.

• To enhance the chi that can lead to greater family harmony, install a low clay or plaster statue, surrounded by the colour yellow, in the south-west.

• For greater peace and tranquillity, a glass statue with a flowing shape is ideal in the north.

• To increase the fire chi associated with fame, public recognition and passion, position a star-shaped or pyramidal statue in the south, with purple flowers around it.

TREES AND PLANTS

> **BENEFIT** Introduces move living chi

Trees and plants help to define the atmosphere of your garden. In general, a well-stocked front garden with a variety of plants carries a healthy balance of chi. You can adjust this to suit your particular needs. The main consideration is how you want to feel in your garden. Use the following ideas to help you with your garden design.

What you do

• An orchard or group of trees creates a space where chi flows vertically. This is a good place to be when you want to focus on yourself and feel more independent.

• An open garden with a large lawn allows chi to move easily around and into your home. This is ideal if you want to feel more outgoing, sociable and active. It could also help you develop bigger ideas, be more open-minded and broaden your vision.

• A more complex layout – where a labyrinth of different plants forces the chi to move in a more convoluted route around plants, flower beds, bushes, trees and curved paths – creates a more imaginative atmosphere, where you may feel more creative, artistic and thoughtful. This is ideal for encouraging new original ideas, feeling more inspired and being able to retreat into your own world.

Trees change the chi on a higher plane, influencing the chi above your head. Sitting under a tree helps you feel different as the tree's chi enters your crown chakra.

• Spiky plants, such as yuccas and palms, create a more exciting atmosphere in your garden, whereas plants with large, floppy leaves generate a calmer feeling. You can select your plants to adjust the way you feel in your garden.

• If you want greater privacy or live near a busy road, it helps to grow a hedge to slow down the chi and act as a barrier to fast-flowing chi.

CONSERVATORIES

BENEFIT Feeling closer to nature

A conservatory has a unique atmosphere, because it lies somewhere between being part of your home and part of the garden. It therefore has a very natural chi, where you feel a strong connection to nature while being protected from the elements. Wherever possible, use natural materials in the conservatory and allow plenty of space for plants. Here are a few things to consider when planning a conservatory.

What you do

1 Try to catch as much sunlight as possible and build the conservatory facing a sunny direction. If your conservatory catches the sunlight for most of the day, you will be able to use it for greater periods. However, conservatories can become very hot, so it is helpful to use vines, creeping plants or a tree to provide shade during the summer. In addition incorporate a system of internal blinds.

2 The materials you use influence the atmosphere of your conservatory. If your conservatory faces east, south-east or south, use wood wherever possible, whereas metal and stone are better if it faces south-west or west.

3 When you add a conservatory to your home, you change the shape of your floor plan. The ideal floor plan for your whole home is as square as possible, so that each of the eight directions is well represented. Some homes have a floor plan where the proportions are such that only a few of the eight directions are represented, while the others are missing. This is typical of a narrow home or one that has an L-shape. It is therefore helpful to add the conservatory in a way that balances the shape; try not to add it in a way that makes the situation worse.

To make your conservatory work, use natural materials and fill it with plenty of plants so you can absorb nature's chi there.

FENG SHUI AND YOUR SPIRITUAL LIFE

NURTURE YOUR SPIRITUAL BEING

The appropriate chi in your home can help you get in touch with your deepest spiritual chi, running through your chakras. At the same time, by accessing your deepest chi and projecting it into your home, you can fill it with the kind of energy that makes it easier to feel spiritual each time you come home.

Meditation and prayer naturally fill your home with this kind of spiritual chi. The whole process will occur more actively if you are doing something that involves movement and takes up more space within your home. For this reason spiritual exercises, such as 'chi gong' (see page 366), can be effective.

This section looks at ways in which you can create a more spiritual environment at home.

• Begin by creating the space to make it easier to access your most spiritual chi. This chi should be slightly dispersed, slow but free-flowing, and should have a vertical component.

• One method to help bring about the right mood is to set up your own personal feng shui temple, so that you can better connect with your own spirituality.

• Look at ways in which you can change your internal chi, making it easier to bring it to the surface.

• Find ways to radiate this spiritual chi out into the space around you by exploring breathing and meditation techniques to project your chi.

• Use chi gong exercises to liberate your chi and allow it to find its own natural ebb and flow within your energy field. Let this chi float out into the room, helping to free up the chi around you.

Salt tends to absorb chi, making it ideal for getting rid of old chi and letting fresh new chi in.

• Employ space-clearing techniques to disperse, refresh and change the chi in your home, making it easier to refill it with your own spiritual energy. You can use sounds to ripple through your home, vibrating the chi and bringing movement to any old energy that has become stagnant.

• Consciously project positive thoughts out into your home, so that you contribute to building a happier atmosphere there.

CREATE THE SACRED SPACE TO BE SPIRITUAL

> **BENEFIT** Finding it easier to feel spiritual

Your spiritual chi not only fills your body, but expands to fill the chi around you. This outer chi interacts with the chi of the space you are thinking in, with the result that the atmosphere around you may make it easier or harder to feel spiritual. Here are some ideas to consider when you are trying to create the ultimate space in which to feel spiritual.

What you do

1 To feel spiritual and allow your mind to fully expand into all the possibilities that are open to you, you need space around your head. If the room is too small, over-furnished or cluttered, your mental chi will be limited in how far it can reach out for new spiritual inspiration before becoming contaminated by other forces.

2 Remember that the chi around you should be clean, and you need to avoid being within stagnant chi, which will stifle your spirituality. Similarly if the chi is tired and has been stuck in the same place, you will find it harder to sense the kind of purity that you need to feel spiritual.

3 Bear in mind that any space with good exposure to fresh air and sunshine will have naturally refreshed and renewed chi. Here you will find it easier to access your spiritual energy.

4 Don't forget that the quickest and most dramatic way to clean the chi of a space is to give it a

complete springclean. Even the process of doing this will clean out your chi, making it easier to access that feeling of purity.

Let fresh chi into your home daily and let some of your old chi out. This can help you feel slightly empty making it easier to reach your spiritual side.

5 As you do your springclean, try to get rid of any unwanted clutter. Too much clutter restricts the movement of chi, making it harder to keep it fresh. More open space makes it easier to disperse chi and avoid congestion.

6 Use tall plants to create a more vertical flow of chi, helping you to connect with the heavens more easily.

SET UP YOUR OWN PERSONAL FENG SHUI TEMPLE

BENEFIT Accesses your spirituality

You can create a special place in your home to serve as your personal feng shui temple. This would be somewhere you go when you want to focus on yourself and ask questions about your life and what your direction is. It could also be somewhere you go to feel a sense of peace and tranquillity, and to get the space between yourself and everyday life that will enable you to be more objective.

What you do

1 Find a room in your home, or a space within a room, that you can dedicate to yourself. Arrange the space so that you face north for greater spirituality, or north-west for wisdom, while you look at the table on which you have created your temple.

2 Bring into this space all the things that are really important to you and which, in your opinion, define who you are and – more importantly – who you want to be.

3 Set these items on your table so that you can get a sense of your place in life's journey so far. They might include pictures, toys, certificates, photographs of your ancestors, old diaries, your favourite books, DVDs or CDs.

4 Also put on the table any affirmations you have made concerning changes that you want to make about yourself, or goals that you want to achieve in life.

5 Place a candle, a bowl of fresh water and a dish of sea salt on the table. When you want to think freely about your life, light the candle and stare into it while you try to empty your mind. Let the chi of your feng shui temple flow into your energy field so that new, unconscious thoughts can enter your mind.

Collect objects and images that mean a lot to you to create your own personal temple. Use this to recharge yourself.

CHANGE YOUR CHI INTERNALLY

BENEFIT Frees up the spirit inside you

In this exercise you learn how to move your chi with your mind. The principle is that by focusing your mind on parts of your body and using positive imagery, you can send helpful chi to those cells.

What you do

1 Find a space that you feel comfortable in and that you think has good natural chi, because you will take in more energy during and at the end of this exercise. Wear loose cotton clothing.

2 Begin by lying comfortably on your back. Use cushions or rolled-up towels under your neck, lower back and knees, if necessary, to make you feel comfortable. Start by breathing slowly and deeply into your abdomen.

3 Imagine you are breathing chi into your abdomen. Move around your body with your mind, asking questions of each place so that you really get to know your body. It is important to find out if each place is relaxed or tense, energetic or tired, hot or cold, hard or soft, and heavy or light. The more you can feel and keep

your attention in a particular place, the stronger the charge of chi to those cells will be.

4 Create an imaginary set of hands that can get inside your body to massage, soothe and generally move chi around. You can invent a colour that makes you feel really good. For example, try a warm gold, orange or yellow. As you take your mind around your body, saturate each part in your special colour. This will bring your powers of visualization to bear on your chi and will affect all the cells within you.

5 Take you mind slowly around your whole body. Then take a few seconds to see how you feel all over. You should feel lighter and more relaxed, with a general sense of harmony.

Make sure you are comfortable and able to fully relax without distractions before beginning your meditation.

RADIATE YOUR CHI INTO A SPACE

BENEFIT Fills a room with your spiritual chi

The aim of this exercise is to develop within you the kind of chi you wish to fill your home with, and then project it into a room, creating a more spiritual atmosphere. You need to do this on a regular basis, as some of your chi will wash away over time.

Sitting with your back to a tree merges your chi field with that of the tree, encouraging your chi to move vertically through your chakras.

What you do

1 Find a place where you can fill your chi field with the kind of energy that helps you feel spiritual – a place of worship, a tree, park, or garden might have the right atmosphere. Whilst there, meditate on your breathing; focus on the in-breath, imagining that you are drawing in the surrounding chi as you fill your lungs. Visualize breathing in a colour, sound or feeling. You might breathe in your favourite colour and imagine your abdomen and chest turning into that colour.

2 Return home and sit with a straight back in the room that you want to fill with more spiritual chi. This time meditate more strongly on the out-breath. Each time you breathe out, imagine your chi filling the room or space you are in. You can begin by filling in a small space around you, then slowly work up to filling a larger and larger space.

3 It will help to place a lit candle in front of you and stare into the flame as you meditate. Concentrate on projecting your chi into the root of the flame as you breathe out, so that the chi of the candle helps radiate your own chi out into the rest of the room more strongly.

BREATHING

> **BENEFIT** Connects you to the chi around you

Every in-breath you take brings chi into your body, and every out-breath expels chi back into the atmosphere. The act of breathing connects you deeply with the chi around you, as the external chi follows the path of the oxygen into your bloodstream. Breathing is the prime way in which you integrate yourself with the world around you. It sets up a rhythmic ebb and flow of chi in and out of your energy field. Your breathing pattern while you are at home will enable you to become more strongly immersed in the chi of your living space.

The way you breathe defines how the process of mixing with the ambient chi takes place. Being able to breathe fully will help you exchange your chi more actively with the chi around you. This is useful when you want to take in more energy from a particular place. For example, you might want to bring in more natural chi from your favourite outdoor location, or to find a public building that has an atmosphere in which you really feel happy.

What you do

1 Practise breathing fully by initially breathing into your abdomen. It can help to put your hand over your navel and concentrate on pushing it away from you as you breathe in. Then tighten your stomach muscles as you breathe out, to expel the air.

2 Once you feel comfortable breathing into your abdomen, continue breathing into your chest. Open your shoulders so that you inhale the maximum possible amount of air.

3 Hold your breath for about three seconds before expelling all the air from your body. You may find that it helps to lean forward slightly and tighten your abdomen, to get all the air out.

Deep breathing by the sea means you take in the sea's chi connecting you to the currents of global energy, helping you think about life in the biggest terms.

MEDITATION

BENEFIT The ability to move chi

The aim of these exercises is to be able to change your energy field with your mind. The key way to control your chi is by moving it down, up, outwards or inwards. This can be achieved by combining breathing, movement and thought in meditation exercises.

What you do

• Move your chi down to become more practical, realistic and grounded; this is ideal if there is too much going on in your head and you cannot get any peace of mind. Breathe out, letting the air out of your chest and then out of your abdomen. Hold the last drop of air in the lowest part of your abdomen until the end. As you breathe out, get a feeling of momentum, so that you can carry on breathing chi down your legs and into your feet, eventually pushing it deep down into the earth below.

• To get new ideas, creative energy and inspiration, move your chi up; this helps you feel positive and like making things happen. Stand with your feet shoulder-width apart, with your weight over the balls of your feet. Start by breathing into the deepest part of your abdomen, and then into your chest. Breathe out by emptying your abdomen and finally letting the last drop of air out of your upper chest. Imagine that you are breathing chi from deep in your abdomen up into your head.

• If you want to be noticed or make an impression, you need to project and expand your chi field outwards; this is ideal for expressing yourself and getting rid of various emotions. Crouch with your feet apart and your arms folded across your chest, and breathe in. As you breathe out, rise and open your arms so that you finish in a star shape. During your out-breath imagine that you are breathing your chi out to the tips of your fingers and toes.

• Draw your chi inwards to develop inner strength, concentrating your deepest core of chi and making it easier to find the power within; try this when you are feeling tired, cold or fragile. Sit or kneel, and breathe in slowly. Start by drawing chi into your abdomen, and then up into your chest. Once your body is full, clench your anus, keeping your mouth and nasal air passages closed as you tighten and pull your abdomen in.

Keeping your back straight aligns all your chakras in a way that makes it easier for chi to flow between them and charge them with chi from the heavens and earth.

CHI GONG

> **BENEFIT** Releases emotions and chi

Chi gong is the art of moving your chi in a way that brings a natural harmony to your whole energy field. To do this, your body is encouraged to make its own spontaneous movements to redistribute, expel or absorb chi. The idea is that your subconscious will know what you really need and that, by getting into a state where your subconscious takes over, you will be able to make the correct adjustments. While you do your chi gong exercises, your extended energy field will make changes to the chi of the room. If you can spontaneously harmonize your own chi, you will simultaneously provoke a spontaneous realignment of the chi in the room.

What you do

To do this you need to prepare your body so that it is easier to begin the spontaneous chi gong movements. The initial exercises are all aimed at freely moving a part of your body without using the muscles there. This helps you relax and open up to letting parts of your body move without using your conscious mind.

Loosen up exercise

1 Shake yourself like a dog. Use your torso to encourage your arms to flop around. With the aid of something to hold onto (a chair back, for instance), shake each leg out, one at a time. Then lie on your back to precipitate free-rocking movements, wriggling your hips so that your arms and legs move without using any of their muscles.

Stimulate your outer chi field

1 To move and play with the periphery of your chi field, run your hands all around your body, keeping them a distance of about 30 cm (1 ft) from your skin.

2 With your feet apart, start by bending down and drawing a circle around your feet. Bring your hands up the sides of your legs and body to your armpits. Then extend your arms out fully. Turn your palms over and bring them towards your neck. Run your hands up the sides of your head and stretch them above your head, before running them down the front of your body until you reach your feet again.

3 Next, run your hands up the back of your legs and torso. When you get to the point where your hands can go no higher behind your back, bring them through to your front under your armpits, and then round the back of your head. Now bring them down the sides of your body, back to your feet. You can now continue by going up the front of your body, starting a new sequence so that you cover every side of your body in each direction.

4 Once you have mastered the basic pattern of movement, you can speed up the whole process, turning it into a vigorous workout. As you do this you will be stirring up your surface chi, mixing it with the chi around you more actively.

Tree hugging exercise

The imagery of this exercise is that you are standing with your front against a large tree with your arms around the trunk. The aim is to find a position in which you can remain like this for as long as possible.

1 Stand with your feet apart and bend your knees by about 15 degrees. You need to tilt your pelvis until you find a comfortable position. Relax your shoulders and put your arms into the tree-hugging position. Tuck your chin in, so that your head feels balanced on your neck. As you stand in this position, be aware of any discomfort and make adjustments until you find a better pose. It is important to remember the stance you develop so that you can begin with it next time. The aim is to learn from the exercise so that you can develop the knowledge and experience to be able to stand for hours in this position.

2 Once you have found the position that works for you, you should have achieved a stance in which your chi can circulate effortlessly. By adopting this position you will be able to free up your chi field and let it resettle in a

more harmonious way. Getting this right takes patience and it helps to have someone else watching you adjust your posture, or to do this in front of a mirror.

Release exercises

The biggest step is to try to allow yourself to initiate spontaneous chi gong movements. First, work on the exercises you have already tried for a few weeks, so that your body is ready for the next step. As you do them, try to cultivate the feeling of letting go completely.

There are two spontaneous options – one standing, and the other lying down – for you to try, to see which suits you best. The advantage of doing this when you are standing is that you have the greatest freedom of movement. However, you might find it easier to start by lying on your back. It can be easier to relax and let go in this position. In either case you may be able to accentuate the movements by breathing out and making a sound while focusing your mind on that part of your body that is moving. Do this completely naturally and let whatever sound comes out happen spontaneously.

At the outset you can get the help of a chi gong master, to make it easier to get started and to watch over you as you let your subconscious take over for a while. It is important to find someone you trust and feel comfortable with. With such a tutor you may find it easier to let go, in the knowledge that there is someone there to look after you.

Standing option

1 When the time feels right, at the end of your chi gong exercises try to spark off subconscious movements by standing in a relaxed stance and stepping back, so that your rear foot only has its toes and the ball of the foot on the ground. Begin by letting your

foot bounce on the ball of your foot. For a while just let this bouncing develop into a natural movement. Try to keep your mind as empty as possible by focusing on your breathing. Let your foot do its own thing.

2 Without thinking about it too much, see if you can let the movement from your foot spread into other areas of your body. This could spark off any kind of rhythmic movement around any joints in your body. The difficulty is to prevent your mind from taking over and starting to make conscious decisions about which joints you want to move and how. It helps to be open to the idea that it might not be the right time – in which case do not force it. Just keep presenting your body with the opportunity and, when the time is right, it will happen naturally. Another option is to swap feet and see if this helps trigger a reaction.

Lying down option

1 Lie on your back and start twitching your hips rhythmically. Let them rotate, twist, tilt or do whatever feels right at the time. Breathe deeply and keep your mind on your breathing. You may find that after a while your legs, arms or neck start moving. Again, just focus your attention on your breathing and resist the temptation to let your mind take over. Once the spontaneous movements have started, you do not need to remain lying on your back. Feel free to lie on your side or to change position completely.

2 After a while you should feel the movements subside. Then you should relax and remain still until you feel completely settled again.

SPACE-CLEARING WITH SOUNDS

> **BENEFIT** Brings in fresh chi

To clear the chi in a space you can use sound. The sound waves ripple outwards through the air, stirring up the chi. If the old chi is free to move, some of it will then flow out of the room, leaving space for more fresh chi to enter.

There are several ways to do this. You can chant, ring bells or clap. Chanting is a powerful option as you project your own deepest chi into the room. It is often helpful to follow up space-clearing with sounds by using sea salt to clean up any leftover chi.

Other sounds – whether music, a gong, or even people talking – will also stir up the chi. The difference is that by using the following methods you can focus the sounds into a specific area and, in the case of chanting, put your own personal chi into it.

What you do

1 Prepare the room you want to clear by opening all the windows and doors and giving it a tidy-up and clean. Concentrate on getting as much dust as possible out of the room. Wear loose cotton clothing as you do this.

2 When you chant, it is important to keep your back straight so that all your chakras line up, making it easier for your chi to flow vertically. To do this, bring your lower ribs back while keeping your shoulders in the same position, so that you straighten your lower back. Tuck your chin in and raise the top of your head, as though your crown is being pulled up to the sky.

3 Breathe in deep breaths so that you can make a long, powerful sound and really project the vibration strongly into the

Singing bowls make a sound you can use to stir up the chi in a room and clear out old stagnant energy.

room. To stir up all the chi in a room, try making a range of sounds. It is easiest to start with a low sound and then work up through the range in one long out-breath. Start with the lowest 'aah' sound, then go to a higher-pitched 'aah' sound; work up through the range of 'ooo' sounds, and finally end with an 'mmm' sound – all in one breath. Do this several times to clear the room. You can use any sound or even sing. However, it will help if you can combine the sound with a long, powerful out-breath and focus on getting your chi out into the room.

4 Remember that hand bells are another useful way to stir up stagnant chi. If you think your room is feeling flat, take a hand bell and ring it in all the corners – and anywhere that dust usually collects. The sound waves will help get the chi moving again and will encourage fresh chi energy into those areas.

5 Another option is to clap your hands smartly while letting out a powerful, quick breath, to get chi moving more quickly. You can combine this with your chanting.

6 Afterwards you can cleanse the chi energy of a space using sea salt, which will soak up any residual chi. Before you go to bed, sprinkle sea salt on the floor in any area of the room that you feel still needs cleansing. In the morning vacuum or sweep up the salt, then take it outside straight away so that you get rid of the negative energy. Repeat this several times until you feel the chi has been refreshed.

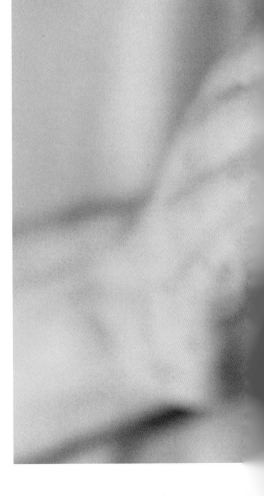

Clapping your hands makes a sound and also sends out your own chi with that sound, especially when combined with a strong out breath.

BRING IN HAPPINESS

> **BENEFIT** Feeling happy at home

The more happy experiences you have at home, the more your home becomes a happy place to be. As the chi of laughter, joy and contentment spills out into the rooms of your home, it becomes part of the atmosphere. This has a cumulative effect, whereby the more consistent you are, and the longer you do this, the greater and more permanent the influence.

You can set all this back if you get seriously depressed, stressed or resentful at home. The risk is that this chi could remain there, making it harder to feel positive again. This is why it is helpful to employ space-clearing techniques (see pages 372–375) after an emotional upset.

It is important to try and fill your home with items that make you happy. Photographs, paintings and sculptures can all be chosen to make it easier to feel content there. You can use music, comedy and colour to bring more laughter and joy into a space.

Other people bring their own chi into your home and, if they feel happy, their positive chi radiates out into the chi of your house or apartment. This is especially true of children. When they are full of joy, they tend to project their chi strongly and actively into the space around them. A contented pet can have the same positive effect on the atmosphere of your home.

As time goes by, you can reach a state where just going home gives you a lift and you feel happier as soon as you soak up the atmosphere there.

Happy people send out happy chi into the atmosphere leaving a happy impression on the room.

What you do

• Use laughter as an excellent way to bring a more joyful, happy chi into your home. Try watching comedies that make you laugh out loud. Similarly, you may have books that amuse you. Jokes, funny games or anything that makes you giggle will lift the atmosphere of your whole home.

• Invite round people with whom you can have fun. Entertaining close friends regularly, playing games and doing things together fills your home with more sociable, vibrant chi.

• If you have children, try to play games with them and encourage them to find things to laugh about. Invite their friends round and let them run wild, if you have the space. Try to eat together so that you come together as a family and share the comical moments of life. If you live on your own, you might find that a pet can bring positive emotions into your home. For this to work, it needs to be a happy environment for your pet.

• Add flowers to bring colour and life into a home, giving it a brighter,

upward-moving chi. Try making big, bold, colourful flower arrangements so that your home thrives on their energy. Similarly, you can plant a variety of flowering plants in one large pot so that your room is awash with colour and living chi.

• Look around your home at all the pictures and artworks to see if they produce a positive response. See if you can find new imagery that makes you smile a little more than the items you already have. Anything that is too dark or sombre, or that reminds you of unhappy times, should be replaced.

• Play music often so that melodic sound waves fill your home. Choose music that you know lifts your spirits and helps you to feel happier.

• Try to find something in every day that provides that special moment – something that you can look forward to as your treat.

• Think about fun hobbies that you can do at home – anything that will help.

Flowers can project a happy colourful chi into your home. Cut the stems and change the water daily to keep them fresh.

MAKE FENG SHUI A PART OF YOUR LIFE

BENEFIT Keeps your feng shui practice alive

Having read this book, you can now begin to use feng shui regularly in your life. Try to use your new concepts of chi, yin and yang, the five elements and the eight directions as fresh ways of looking at the world around you. The more you can make feng shui a part of your everyday life, the more you can integrate it naturally into everything you do. Eventually feng shui should be something that is intuitively inside you, rather than an abstract concept. In this sense you need to make it yours.

What you do

1 Work on your own chi using meditation and exercise and by eating whole 'living' foods.

2 Keep looking at things in terms of yin and yang, and try to make connections between the way you feel and the many outside influences on you.

3 When you visit friends, see if you can connect aspects of their characters and lives with the feng shui of their homes.

4 Consider enrolling on a feng shui course if you wish to take things further.

5 Find out people's dates of birth and look up their feng shui astrology numbers, then keep making associations between their three numbers and their characters.

6 Try out feng shui astrology on different people you know by making a chart comparing their year, month and axis numbers.

By sitting at this table you will be able to absorb and sense the bright, colourful chi and experience how this makes you feel.

7 Use feng shui astrology to work out the different phases of various friends or family members during their lives. See if your predictions match their real-life experiences.

8 Try out some of the feng shui remedies on your own home and then, if you have willing friends, gain useful experience by applying the feng shui in this book to their lives and homes.

PUT IT ALL INTO PERSPECTIVE

BENEFIT Greater harmony

Remember that everything in this book is based on concepts and not on a rigid reality. You may find that applying these concepts to your life has amazing results, but it is important to see feng shui as just one piece of the jigsaw puzzle of life. There are many other concepts to explore and try out.

Try to keep feng shui in perspective so that it complements other aspects of your life, while providing you with an abundance of new, interesting ideas

for your home. Use feng shui to help you make more informed choices. In the end, feng shui is just another tool that can assist you on your life's journey. It can make the journey more interesting and help you through those difficult patches. But it is not a magic pill and does not provide a foolproof solution to anything. Instead, it is a skill that you can use in order to do more with less effort. And hopefully it can lead to a more fulfilling life.

What you do

1 Try not let this subject (or any other) limit your life, but use it to empower yourself. You should still be in control and living the life you desire, while using feng shui to make it better.

2 Make the effort to understand everything, so that you know what you are doing. Avoid doing anything in blind faith, so that you do everything from a position of strength.

3 When making changes to your life, make one change at a time so that you can monitor the results. The risk of rushing in and making wholesale changes is that you will not know what is working and what is not.

4 Practise and get as much experience as you can with every aspect of feng shui, so that you can test it through your own participation and reinforce everything you have learnt in this book with real-life experience.

Keep notes or a diary to connect the way you feel with the spaces you spend time in. Looking back, this can be a valuable personal resource.

GLOSSARY

Aura: An energy field that surrounds the human body. It can be photographed using a process called Kirlian photography, whereby it shows up as a multi-coloured haze. With practice you can see the aura with your eye or feel it with your hands.

Ba gua: *See* Magic square.

Chakras: Seven points or activity centres along the body where your chi is particularly active. They are: the spiral at the top of your head, the area between your eyebrows, your throat, the area between your nipples, your stomach, just below your navel and the base of your spine. The chakras are often used in healing to create a more healthy flow of chi around your body.

Chi: A subtle electromagnetic energy that flows through everything, passing on information from one entity to another. It is as though everything is linked by an invisible network, so that you influence – and are influenced by – everything you know. In the human body, chi carries your thoughts, ideas and emotions. This energy extends beyond your body, enveloping you with your own chi energy field. You can see chi using Kirlian photography. It is easy to influence chi through the atmosphere of your home – this is why you feel different in different places.

Chi field: The energy that forms your own personal chi. This is within you, but also fills an area around you, ranging from a few centimetres (a couple of inches) from your skin to 1 m (3 ft), depending on how strongly you are projecting your chi at the time.

Chi gong: Spiritual exercises that liberate your chi and allow it to find its own natural ebb and flow within your energy field.

Eight directions: Eight points of the compass that are used to build up a character for the different sorts of energy found in each of these directions. For example, the energy of the east is associated with sunrise, the morning and spring; this might be a helpful energy to absorb into your own chi field if you want that get-up-and-go feeling. Conversely, the sunset energy of the west is associated with the autumn harvest time and the end of the day; this is better for completing things properly or for reaping the rewards of your hard work. Once you know what of each of the eight directions has to offer, you can use feng shui to bring more of that particular energy into your being.

Feng shui: Literally translates as 'wind and water'. The way these elements move around the planet is much the same as the flow of feng shui energy – they both form a connection with the outside world and with your body. Humans are 70 per cent water, and the water inside you is constantly being replenished by fresh water from outside, in a similar way that you take in oxygen from the air. Wind and water are your most vital links to your environment – without either you would soon die. Feng shui is based on the same idea, but focuses on an energy that carries information about you, and constantly blends and updates it with energy from the world around you.

Five animals: These represent your outer energy field; they are positioned around your body and always take the same positions. The energy in front of you is represented by the phoenix, to your right by the tiger, to your rear by the tortoise, to your left by the dragon and in the centre by the snake.

Five elements: The five different kinds of emotional energy represented by the elements of wood, fire, soil, metal and water. Each energy is associated with a time of day and a season, and this is the easiest way to get a feel for them. Imagine being out in nature at a certain time of the day and year: wood = sunrise and spring; fire = midday and summer; soil = afternoon and summer changing to autumn; metal = sunset and autumn; water = midnight and winter. The most important aspect of the five elements is the way in which they relate to each other. This forms the basis of working out why there might be problems in a home and how to solve them.

Magic square: An arrangement of the numbers 1–9 on a grid, so that any three in a straight line always add up to 15. Each number is either more yin or yang than the next number, and has an associated element and trigram. This grid is laid over your house plan to see the flow of energy there. Feng shui is based on Fu Hsi's magic square (also known as the ba gua). When applied to a home, the magic square is arranged in its standard form, with the number 5 in the centre (see page 42).

Meridians: Paths that carry chi energy around your body. They feed smaller branches, until your chi reaches every cell in your body. This means that every thought and emotion will touch every cell, and over the long term this can affect your physical body – so think twice before launching into another rage or depression. The reverse is also true: the condition of your cells and the way you use your body alter the way your energy flows and the way you think and feel. You may have noticed that it is very hard to remain angry if you breathe slowly and stretch out, or to get depressed if you are in the middle of vigorous exercise.

Nine ki system: A system based on the magic square, where each of the nine numbers describes a type of chi. The numbers can be arranged in nine different ways on the magic square, to create a cycle of nine that may be applied to years, months or days. This can then be used to work out the chi present when someone was born, plus the best directions and phases in each year and month.

Space-clearing: Techniques – ranging from cleaning and getting rid of clutter, through ringing bells, chanting and clapping hands, to meditation – that are used to disperse old stagnant chi from a space.

Trigrams: A series of three parallel lines, either solid or broken. Broken lines are more yin, and solid lines are more yang. There are eight different arrangements of these lines, and each is linked to one of the eight directions.

Year number, month number and axis number: Three numbers, from 1 to 9, that represent the chi inside you, based on the year and month in which you were born. The axis number is a combination of your year and month numbers (to find your axis number, look at the magic square with your month number in the centre, then find your year number and see in which direction it lies; the number normally associated with that direction – when 5 is in the centre of the magic square – is your axis number). Each number describes a particular type of chi, and this can be used to look at your character and relationships. In addition, your year number can be used to work out the phase you are in each year and month, as well as which directions are best for you.

Yin and yang: These are opposite and complementary terms that can be used to describe anything. The literal translation is that yin represents the shady side of the mountain, and yang the sunny side. Generally yang refers to anything that makes you active, energetic, quick, alert, focused, precise, aggressive, assertive or tense. Yin describes anything that helps you relax, slow down, open your mind, be creative, stimulate your imagination, be flexible and easy-going, look at the big picture and be receptive. One thing is always more yin or yang than something else. For example, doing karate makes you more yang than stretching, but stretching is more yang than having a snooze. You can therefore decide whether you feel happier being more yin or yang, and then adjust your lifestyle to make this happen. Yin and yang can be applied to the decoration of your home, the food you eat, the clothes you wear or any of your activities.

INDEX

A

animals
  and best directions 59
  five animals 10, 34–5, 209, 300,
    386
arguments 278, 282–3, 288–9
artwork 167, 379
  and creativity 201, 220–1
astrology *see* magic square; nine ki
  numbers
aura 14, 26, 384

B

ba gua *see* magic square
babies 278, 302–3
balconies 338–9
bathrooms 133, 134–5
beams 137, 165
bedrooms 126, 173
  beds and bedding 140–1, 183
  and sex 172, 180, 182–3
  see also sleeping directions
bells 91, 273, 274, 275
bereavement 306–7
best directions 58–61
  for careers and businesses 326–7
blinds 202–3
breathing 352, 362–3
  and meditation 201, 214–15

business cycles, nine ki 54
businesses, starting new 325

C

candles 86, 148, 156–7, 274
  in the bedroom 182, 183
careers 309–27
  best direction for 326–7
  computers 320–1
  creating a launch pad 312–13
  desks 310, 316–17
  directional qualities 314–15, 324–5,
    326–7
  and feng shui astrology 311
  home offices 310–11
  imagery 322–3
  important career changes 324–5
  office chairs 318–19
  sitting positions 314–15
cars 258, 259
chairs 160, 161, 169, 300, 301
  in offices 310, 318–19
chakras 14, 26–7, 365
  and sleeping directions 138–9
chanting 274, 372, 373, 374
charcoal 85, 243, 289
chi 9, 13, 14–15, 24–9, 384
  arriving through windows and doors
    122–3

bringing in happiness 376, 379
and candles 156–7
and careers 313, 314, 316, 317
chi field 385
and creativity 201
establishing the prevailing type 121
and families 278, 279, 280–1, 292
    bringing in missing chi 286–7,
        289
and finances 238–9, 240–1, 242
and the five animals 34–5
and the five elements 30–3
and floor plans 116–17
and footprints 119
and health 126–7
and moving home 250, 252–3,
    254–5, 262–3, 266
    pollution 260–1
    rituals 273
and nature 330–1, 332–3, 335,
    345
and the nine numbers 36–41, 93
nine patterns of 43
in relationships 172–3, 178–9, 186
    bringing in missing chi 178–9
south-western 185
and sharp edges 164
and space clearing with sounds
    372–5
and spiritual life 354–5
    changing your chi internally 358–9
    radiating into a space 360–1

and utility rooms 294–5
and water 132–3
and windows 122–3, 262
    see also yin and yang
chi gong exercises 352, 366–71, 385
children 378
children's rooms 279, 304–5
Chinese culture 18
Chinese influence 13–14
circular rooms 158–9
clocks 84
clothing 186, 187
clutter 149, 201, 222–3, 355
colours
    and creativity 204, 205
    and finances 230–1, 238, 239
    flowers 190
    and home design 68–9
    mood-changing 148, 150–1
    and moving home 275
    and relationships 183, 185, 194–5,
        197
compass and non-compass feng shui
    20, 22
computers
    and electromagnetic fields 143
    keeping plants near 142
    using to make floor plans 108
    working with 320–1
confidentiality 102
conservatories 331, 348–9
cookers 129

cooking methods 131
corners 165
creativity 198–225
    and artwork 201, 220–1
    and clutter 201, 222–3
    designing a creative atmosphere
        200–1
    getting out of the house 208–9
    and loft spaces 212–13
    meditation and breathing 201,
        214–15
    and mirrors 201, 218–19
    and open spaces 200, 206–7
    and patterns 200, 204–5
    and sound waves 201, 224–5
    and time of day/month 210–11
    and windows 200, 202–3
crystals 89, 183, 246
cultural differences 18
curtains 202
curved forms 149, 166–7
cushions 68, 160, 169

D

dining areas 292–3
discretion 102
divination 100–1
doors
    chi arriving through 122–3
        and plants 136–7
    and finances 236, 237

E

eight directions 58–61, 385
    and colours 69
    and creativity 207, 216–17, 218
    and finances 233, 234–5
    and floor plans 112–17
    school of feng shui 23
    transparency 112–13, 119, 185,
        207, 216, 218, 231, 326
eight mansions school of feng shui 22,
    23
eight trigrams 10, 13, 19, 387
electromagnetic fields (EMFs) 142–3,
    250, 258, 260, 305
    and office equipment 310, 320, 321
emotions, nine ki 55
empty rooms 149
ethics of feng shui 102–3
everyday life, feng shui as part of
    380–1
exercise 197
    chi gong 352, 366–71, 385

F

fabrics 279, 289
    and creativity 200
    curved forms in 167
families 276–306
    arguments 278, 282–3
        reducing 288–9
    bereavement 306–7
    bringing in missing chi 286–7, 289

children's rooms 279, 304–5
colours 281, 289, 290, 291
creating a playful atmosphere 290–1
directional qualities 280, 281, 299,
    302–3
fabrics 279, 289
and feng shui astrology 284–5
kitchens and dining areas 278,
    292–3
living rooms 279, 298–9
nurseries 278, 302–3
plants 289, 290, 305
seating 300–1
sleeping directions 281, 287
storage 296–7
utility rooms 294–5
fees 103
finances 226–47
coins on a red cloth 230–1
directional attributes 233, 234–5
financial flows 246–7
increasing your income 242–3
money plants 232–3
and north-eastern chi 238–9
saving more 244–5
stairs and doors 236–7
starting new ventures 240–1
fireplaces/fires 149, 162–3
fish 131
five animals 10, 34–5, 300, 386
and creativity 209
five elements 10, 13, 30–3, 386

and creativity 205
and the eight directions 117
and families 284, 285, 286, 287
and house shapes 263, 265
lighting 72–3
materials 71
and plants 136
and relationships 173, 176–7,
    178–9
shapes 75
floating candles 157
floor plans 11, 106, 108–19
and conservatories 349
and creativity 207, 218
and the eight directions 112–17
and finances 231
fine-tuning relationships 174
footprints 118–19
and south-western chi 185
flowers 83, 183, 378–9
and relationships 190–1
fluorescent lighting 155
flying star school of feng shui 22–3
focus, finding 99
food 128, 130–1
eating together 188, 189
footprints, establishing in the home
    118–19
form school of feng shui 20–1, 23
fruits 130
Fu Hsi 14, 386
furniture

balconies 339
children's rooms 305
curves in 167
getting the balance right 168–9
influence on mood 149, 160–1

gardens 331, 340–7
hedges 347
paths and sculptures 331, 344–5
planning 340–1
plants 340, 341, 346–7
trees and plants 346–7
water features in 342–3

H
halogen lighting 154
hand bells 91, 273, 274, 275
happiness 376–9
health 124–45
and chi 126–7
keeping your home healthy 127
pollution from toxic fumes 144–5
hedges 347
hills 256–7
home offices 310–11
homes 96, 104–23
chi in 24–5, 116–17, 119, 121
design features 10, 66–77, 86
establishing the facing direction
120–1
and feng shui problems 17
feng shui survey 106

finding your best directions 61
and the magic square 42, 43
and schools of feng shui 20–3
see also floor plans; moving home

I
imagery
and careers 322–3
changing moods with 148, 152–3
in home offices 310
improvements after using feng shui 8–9

K
key concepts 9, 12–63
kinesiology 100, 101
kitchens 126, 127–8, 166, 292–3

L
L-shaped homes 111
lampshades 154
larders 126, 127–8
laughter 378
lighting
changing moods with 148, 154–5
and home design 72–3
kitchens 129
see also candles
living rooms 279, 298–9
location, moving home 254–5
loft spaces, and creativity 200, 212–13
lovers see relationships

M

magic square 10, 14, 42–57, 386
   and the nine patterns of chi 42, 43
   see also nine ki numbers
maps, and the eight directions 60
materials
   in bathrooms 134
   garden paths and sculptures 345
   and home design 70–1
   in kitchens 128
   and moving home 251
mattresses 141
meat 131
meditation 86, 90, 99, 352, 364–5,
   380
   and breathing 201, 214–15
   and creativity 201, 214–15
   and moving home 274
meridians 15, 26, 387
microwave ovens 129
mirrors 87, 195
   and creativity 201, 218–19
   and families 291
mobile phones 143
moods 146–69
   and candles 148, 156–7
   and colour 148, 150–1
   and fires/fireplaces 149, 162–3
   and furniture 149, 160–1
   and imagery 148, 152–3
   and lighting 148, 154–5
   linear and curved forms 149, 166–7

   and room proportions 149, 158–9
moving home 17, 58, 97, 248–75
   blending your home with your
   personality 274–5
   checklist 270–1
   choosing location 254–5
   facing direction 250, 266–7
   floor plans 251
   hills and water 256–7
   moving to a particular direction
      268–9
   and natural light 251, 264–5
   outside 262–3, 271
   railways and roads 258–9
   rituals on moving in 272–3
   surveying the site 264–5
music 379
myths and superstition 18–19

N

nature 97, 328–49
   balconies 338–9
   bringing into your home 334–5
   and chi 330–1, 332–3, 345
   conservatories 331, 348–9
   and plants 331, 334, 335
   spending time outdoors 332–3
   water features 339, 342–3
   window boxes 331, 336–7
   see also gardens
nine ki numbers 42–52, 380–1, 387,
   388

axis numbers 44, 52, 58, 284, 388
  finding 44–9
  meaning of 50–2
  month numbers 44, 51, 53, 58,
    388
  and relationships 173, 176–7
  and the timing of events 53–7,
    192–3
  year numbers 44, 50, 53, 58, 311,
    388
nine types of chi (nine numbers) 23,
  36–41, 93
nurseries 278, 302–3

O

objects
  curved 167
  influence on mood 149, 152, 153
offices see careers
orchids 183
origins of feng shui 12–13

P

pairs, arranging things in 153
paths 331, 344–5
patterns, and creativity 200, 204–5
people, focus on 97
photographs 152, 153, 187, 376
pictures 152, 153, 376, 379
plants 82, 107, 169, 334, 335
  in bathrooms 135, 136–7
  in corners 165

and electromagnetic fields (EMFs)
    142
  and families 289, 290, 305
  flowering 191
  in gardens 340, 341, 346–7
  in kitchens 129
  money plants 232–3
  for reducing pollution 145
  and spirituality 355
  window boxes 336–7
playrooms 279, 304–5
pollution 144–5, 260–1
professionalism 103
promotion, applying for 325
pyramids 12–13

R

railways 258
real-life problems, applying feng shui to
    11
rectangular homes 110
relationships 170–97
  and candles 156, 182, 183
  constructing your relationship chart
    176–7
  eating, sitting and sleeping together
    188–9
  finding a lover 194–5
  fine-tuning 174–5
  and the five elements 173, 176–7,
    178–9
  and flowers 190–1

intimacy and closeness 186–7
making the most of 184–5
mixing your chi with your lover's
    172–3
nine phases of 56–7
remedies 92–3
and sex 172, 180, 182–3
timing of 53, 192–3
when a relationship ends 196–7
remedies 11, 78–93, 96, 98, 381
bells 91, 273, 274, 275
bringing about change 78–9
candles 86
charcoal 85, 243, 289
clocks 84
crystals 89
finding your focus 99
flowers 83
how to use 92–3
meditation 86, 90
mirrors 87
plants 82
sea salt 81, 107, 273, 353, 374
water features 80
wind chimes 88
roads 258–9
roofs 262, 263
room layout 76–7
room proportions 149, 158–9

S

schools of feng shui 9, 20–3
sculptures in gardens 331, 344–5
sea salt 81, 107, 273, 353, 374
seating 149, 163
chairs 160, 161, 169, 300, 301
families 300–1
sitting places 35, 62–3
sexual relationships 172, 180, 182–3
shapes, and home design 74–5
sharp edges, softening 149, 164–5
shrines 306–7
sitting directions 211, 216–17
careers 314–15
sitting places 35, 62–3
skylights 122
sleeping directions 138–9, 180–1,
    194, 197, 244
and families 281, 287
and finances 244, 246
and relationships 180–1, 194, 197
sleeping together 189
small rooms 158
sound waves, and creativity 201,
    224–5
sounds, space-clearing with 372–5
space-clearing 372–5, 387
spiritual life 350–83
breathing 362–3
bringing in happiness 376–9
changing your chi internally 358–9
chi gong 366–71

creating a sacred space 352, 354–5
and meditation 364–5
radiating into a space 360–1
setting up a personal temple 352,
356–7
space-clearing with sounds 372–5
spring-cleaning 354–5
square rooms 158
stairways 137
and finances 236–7
statues in gardens 344
Stone Circles 12
storage 296–7
sunbathing 333
sunlight 335, 349

T
tables 160–1
tall buildings 262, 263
tall rooms 149, 158
teas 131
telephones 143
three-gate school of feng shui 21
timing of events 53–7
relationships 53, 192–3
toilets 135
toxic fumes 144–5, 261
tree hugging 368
trees 346–7
trigrams 10, 13, 19, 387

U
utility rooms 294–5

V
vases 83
vegetables 130–1

W
water 132–3
in the kitchen 128
moving home 256–7
water features 80, 331, 339, 342–3
waterfalls 256, 343
wind chimes 88, 123
window boxes 331, 336–7
windows
and chi 122–3, 262
and plants 136–7
and creativity 200, 202–3
opening 335

Y
yin and yang 10, 13, 28–9, 380, 388
colours 67, 68
lighting 72
materials 67, 70
shapes 74

ABOUT THE AUTHOR

Simon Brown qualified as a design engineer, having two inventions patented in his name. He then began his studies in Oriental medicine in 1981 and qualified as a shiatsu therapist and macrobiotic consultant. While learning these healing arts he studied feng shui with Japanese masters in the United States. Simon was the director of London's Community Health Foundation for seven years, running a wide range of courses specializing in the Oriental healing arts. During this time he organized the first major feng shui courses in the UK. Since 1993, Simon has made feng shui his full-time career. His clients include well-known celebrities such as Boy George and large public companies, including the Body Shop and British Airways. Simon is a member of the Feng Shui Society.

Consultations with Simon G. Brown

Simon provides a complete consultation service. Consultations can be arranged to include a site visit, or they can be done by e-mail or post. They include floor plans with feng shui recommendations, a full report including a survey, explanation of the recommendations, your astrology information for this year and the next three years, your best directions for this year, and the best dates on which to implement the recommendations. Ongoing advice by telephone or e-mail is also included.

Courses with Simon G. Brown

Simon provides a variety of courses, ranging from one-day introductory courses to a full certificate course with homework and an assessment.

Contact details

Simon G. Brown, PO Box 10453, London, NW3 4WD

Tel +44 (0) 20 7431 9897

Fax +44 (0) 20 7431 9897

E-mail simon@chienergy.co.uk

Website www.chienergy.co.uk

Books by Simon G. Brown

Astrology by Numbers

Published by Carroll & Brown, ISBN 1-903258-61-8

Essential Feng Shui

Published by Cassell and Co., ISBN 0-7063-7854-7

Feng Shui in a Weekend

Published by Hamlyn, ISBN 0-600-60378-4

Practical Feng Shui

Published by Cassell & Co., ISBN 0-7063-7634-X

ACKNOWLEDGEMENTS

Acknowledgements

A special thank you to Brenda for commissioning me to write this book, and to Alison it is wonderful to work with you again. I am greatly indebted to my wife, children and mother for all their love and support while I was writing this book. I am also very appreciative of all those who have bought my other books, some of whom I have been in contact with over the years – and of course I am appreciative of you, for reading this book.

Alamy 232; /Image Source 85. **All About Feng Shui**/www.all-about-feng-shui-co.uk 19 top, 19 bottom. **Corbis UK Ltd.** 241, 382; /Ted Horowitz 230. **Getty Images** 252, 276, 279, 304, 374-375; /Tony Anderson 291; /Jim Arbogast 315; /Bruce Ayres 103; /Jim Bastardo 17; /Jean Louis Batt 133; /C Borland/ PhotoLink 120; /Bozena Cannizzaro 142-143; /Chabruken 360; /Martial Colomb 338; /Donna Day 330; /DGP&C 318; /Digital Vision 222-223, 332; /Erik Dreyer 272; /Amy Eckert 63; /Paul Edmondson 263; /Erlanson Productions 292; /Claudia Goetzelmann 283; /Dana Hoff 181, 259; /Seth Joel 208; /Elliott Kaufman 221; /Georgia Kokolis 256; /Microzoa 301; /Giuseppe Molteni 334; /Patrick Molnar 295; /Antony Nagelmann 92; /Junshi Nakamichi 82; /David Oliver 320; /Paul Redman 348; /Trinette Reed 242-243; /Ken Reid 84; /Marc Romanelli 323; /Andersen Ross 134; /Andrea Rugg 217; /Marcus Wilson-Smith 312; /Phillip Spears 267; /Don Spiro 261; /Tim Street-Porter 235; /Stephen Studd 13; /Friedhelm Thomas 299; /Simon Watson 355; /Mel Yates 327; /Yellow Dog Productions 251. **Octopus Publishing Group Limited** 71, 98, 131, 145, 149, 170-171, 195, 204, 219, 308-309, 311, 368;/Mark Bolton/Design: Geoffrey Whiten, RHS Chelsea Flower Show 2001 341; /Mark Bolton/Design: Karen Maskell, Frederick Warne & Co., RHS Hampton Court Flower Show 2001 342; /Peter Pugh-Cook 196, 367, 370, 371, 376; /Colin Gotts 182; /Walter Gardiner 363; /Mike Hemsley 91, 157, 215, 307; /Rupert Horrox 184; /Alistair Hughes 172; /David Loftus 83, 166, 190; /Tom Mannion 74, 80, 94, 124-125, 139, 140, 155, 164, 168, 247, 264-265, 297; /Peter Myers 2, 10, 24, 64-65, 66, 68, 73, 75, 87, 104, 107, 122, 123, 129, 130, 146-147, 148, 150, 152-153, 161, 163, 169, 200-201, 203, 206, 353, 378; /David Parmitter 11, 226-227, 245, 288; /Ian Parsons 81, 86, 89, 101, 240, 275, 356; /Adrian Pope 303; /Mike Prior 358, 365; /William Reavell 135; /Howard Rice 344, 347; /Unit Photographic 317 372; /Ian Wallace 191, 225; /Mark Winwood 239; /Steve Wooster 337; /Jacqui Wornell 88; /Polly Wreford 25, 33, 72, 186, 186-187; /Mel Yates 67, 137, 381. **Imagesource** 78, 96, 174-175, 188, 192. **Papa Architects Ltd**/www.papaarchitects.co.uk (Stockists: +44 (0)20 83488411) 70, 126, 144, 154, 159, 213, 236. **Photodisc** 8. **Science Photo Library**/Garion Hutchings 15. **TopFoto**/Charles Walker 22.

Executive Editor Brenda Rosen
Managing Editor Clare Churly
Executive Art Editor Sally Bond
Designer Patrick McLeavey
Illustrator Ruth Hope, Trevor Bounford, Sally Bond
Picture Library Manager Jennifer Veall
Production Manager Louise Hall